THE BEST WINES IN THE SUPER MARKETS 2012

THE BEST

INES

IN THE

SUPER
MARKETS
2012

NED HALLEY

foulsham
LONDON • NEW YORK • TORONTO • SYDNEY

foulsham

Capital Point, 33 Bath Road, Slough, Berkshire
SL1 3UF, England

Foulsham books can be found in all good bookshops and direct
from www.foulsham.com

ISBN: 978-0-572-03651-5

Text copyright © 2012 Ned Halley
Series, format and layout design © W. Foulsham & Co. Ltd

Cover photograph © Thinkstock

A CIP record for this book is available from the British Library

The moral right of the author has been asserted

Printed and bound in Great Britain by Martins the Printers Ltd

Contents

What's good about the wines in the supermarkets?

After tasting supermarket wines by the thousand for more years than I now wish to count, I am convinced that they are better today than they have ever been. The wines are more diverse in sheer number, and also in terms of location, grape variety, style and price. Go into any supermarket that takes its wines seriously, and you should find something you like, whatever your taste.

I think this is marvellous. Thanks largely to the supermarkets, wine has become an 'everyday' shopping item. We are nearly a wine-drinking nation in the manner of our continental neighbours, now that we get through about 1.8 billion bottles a year. That means every Briton gets through just over half a bottle of wine every week.

Well, put that way maybe it doesn't sound much, but bear in mind that not everyone drinks wine. By the time you've extracted juveniles, teetotallers, and the one third of adults who don't really like wine, the people who do drink it are probably accounting for a whole bottle per week. Just imagine.

It's true that most of the wine is of what might be called incidental quality. By that I mean it's familiar and affordable and, incidentally, it tastes OK. The big names from Australia, California and South Africa that take up so much space on supermarket shelves and behind the counters of pubs and bars do indeed account for the bulk of all wine sales.

Alarms are regularly sounded in the wine trade that these global brands are squeezing out the characterful wines, made on a much smaller scale, that are the perceived soul of the business. But I don't believe a word of it. The wine business is like any other. Give the customers what they want. All of them. Of course, the big chains sell no end of Arniston Bay and Blossom Hill to the customers who want them. That's the great majority of supermarket customers. But the chains also serve their comparatively tiny contingents of dedicated wine enthusiasts with equal energy and determination.

It makes me feel very happy to wander along the wine aisles of a big Asda, Tesco or Waitrose and to contemplate the astonishing choice on offer. I know they had wine lovers like me in mind when they set out to find so much of what is on display. They are catering with enormous generosity to a tiny minority. I am thrilled that the buyer believes I want to choose between a Campania Fiano and a Puglia Falanghina, a Duero or a Douro, a Pouilly-Fumé or a Pouilly-Fuissé.

This isn't in some esoteric cellar far beneath the pavements of St James's in London. This is a few seconds' squeak behind your trolley from the baby food and bog rolls. It is, as I keep telling myself, brilliant.

Not everyone agrees with me. In 2011, Alcohol Concern revealed that it had conducted a survey in four stores – Asda, Morrisons, Sainsbury's and Tesco – and had found that, in the words of the charity's chief executive, Don Shenker: 'It's now common practice to sell wines next to ready meals, pushing the idea that a relaxing meal should be accompanied by an alcoholic drink. Such practices promote alcohol as a normal commodity, like any other type of food or drink.'

To this, Mr Shenker added that 'with 75 per cent of alcohol being purchased by people drinking at hazardous or harmful levels, it is incumbent on retailers to act responsibly. Saturating every aisle of a store with alcohol displays demonstrates once again that big supermarkets are intent on placing their profits above public health.'

I include Mr Shenker's pronouncement on this topic because it is only proper to take a balanced view. But is he right? It is axiomatic that drinking wine with food is the least harmful way to take alcohol on board. There is even evidence that wine taken with food has positive benefits for health. And if it is true that three-quarters of all alcohol is consumed by people hazarding or harming their health by doing so, one can only wonder how many of those are accounted for by supermarket customers who like a glass of wine with their supper.

It is not fashionable to defend the supermarkets, but I believe Mr Shenker does them an injustice by claiming they intend to profit by endangering public health. What sort of people does he think actually work in supermarket retailing?

Time to return to the positive. And let's start with pricing. Be in no doubt that supermarket wines are better value right now than they have ever been. At a time of high overall inflation at around 5 per cent, and with the most punitive alcohol excise rates in the Western world, wine prices have increased only marginally this year over last. The excise on a bottle of table wine rose to £1.81 in the 2011 Budget, just after VAT had been raised to 20 per cent. VAT is payable on excise, so the starting price of a bottle of wine on the shelf is £2.18. And yet there are wines I am happy to recommend in this year's edition that cost as little as £3.39. On that bottle (of Sainsbury's Corbières) the taxes account for £2.35, leaving a shade over a quid to cover everything else including the supermarket's mark-up.

Don't ask me how they do it, especially when wines from the puffed-up euro zone and recovering New World producing countries have to be paid for with our own chronically ailing currency. And yet all the major retailers still persist in discounting large numbers of their wines, all the time. It's true that many of these promotions are cynical scams – you know the sort of thing, a £3.99 wine goes on the shelf for a period at £7.99 and then is 'halved' in price with great fanfare back to £3.99 again – but plenty of wine bargains are the genuine article. In the listings in this edition, I have tried to mention when particular wines have, in the recent past at least, been regularly discounted.

On the whole it is the branded wines that go on price promotion. This is because it's mostly the supplier, rather than the retailer, who funds the discount. It is different with supermarket own-label wines. These are more realistically priced in the first place, partly because you're not paying for the huge cost of brand support. And of course own-label wines are made with the close participation of the retailer, whose price agreement with the supplier is contractual. It's less easy for the supermarket to bully the supplier into funding a price promo on pain of having his wines cleared from the shelves if he doesn't divvy up.

Own-label wines are the true growth area in supermarkets. All the Big Four are extending their ranges, at all sorts of price levels, very busily indeed. Tesco is to launch an entry-price range under the banner 'Simply', in counterpoint to its excellent 'Finest' range, and as a rival to Sainsbury's 2010-launched 'House' wines, which have been an overnight sensation. Morrisons has only just got into gear on this front, but makes an impressive start this year with three distinct ranges. Marks & Spencer, of course, does nothing but own-label wines. The Co-op does fewer than might be expected, but I anticipate there will be more wines under The Co-operative brand in the near future. Waitrose, with the biggest range overall, again has surprisingly few own-labels, sticking to a small selection of 'Waitrose in Partnership' wines. But bear in mind that Waitrose has only relatively recently expanded to its present size. Not much over a decade ago, it was a regional retailer (London and the southeast) with 100-or-so stores. Today, it's a major national operator with 243 supermarkets, planning to extend that network to 400 in the next few years. Own-label wines are only economic when you have scale, and scale is something Waitrose is fast acquiring.

All this is by way of admitting, of course, that supermarkets are taking over the world (and each other). Waitrose is by no means the only chain that is growing at an exponential rate. The Co-op now has 3,000 grocery branches, having absorbed hundreds of small-town stores from the defunct Somerfield. Asda is doing something very similar now that it has swallowed Netto, and we soon forget that Morrisons, once a strictly Yorkshire enterprise, only became the giant it is today by taking over a much larger rival, Safeway.

As these giants consolidate and enlarge, is choice the loser? In wine terms, I don't believe so. Even though the UK's largest high street wine merchant, Thresher/Wine Rack, crashed in 2010 and was followed by the country's best-loved merchant, Oddbins, in 2011, what have wine lovers really lost? The supermarkets may or may not have driven these two companies out of business, but they are certainly doing a good job of filling the void. And independent wine shops, regional merchants and specialist online operators are as much the beneficiaries of the demise of the high street chains as the supermarkets are. Britain remains a natural home for wine lovers, thanks to the sheer diversity of what is on offer from every kind of retailer.

A word about my scoring system in this book. It is strictly relative. Tasting up to 200 wines in a single session, I fix each wine at a point on my likeability/value scale from 0 to 10. Any note with a 6 or above gets typed into the shortlist from which the wines in the following pages are selected. Only a handful of 6- or 7-scoring wines make the cut, because while they are wines I have liked, I have not been convinced on value grounds. It is the 8-scoring wines that make up the greatest number. They are really good wines at what I believe to be fair prices. A score of 9 indicates special interest and value. A score of 10 goes to any wine I have found to be exceptionally delicious, at a completely fair price, or even at what seems to me an unnecessarily low price. In short, a must-try.

Finally, to update you on our online options. Many of you regular readers will have already signed up to the companion website for *The Best Wines in the Supermarkets* – **www.bestwinesuk.net** – so you can use the online search to find the wines you enjoy. Plus, this year, I am trying a new experiment. Inevitably, changes will have taken place between going to press and publication. Prices change, vintages are updated, wines sell out. I'm adding a new feature to appear on the site and also on my own website, **www.nedhalley.com** in which I will be providing readers of this book with regular updates to the listings. I will post any price or other changes I hear about, and where vintages move on I will add notes on the new ones when I have tasted them. And I will endeavour too to highlight listed wines that go on price promotion, and to add any exciting new discoveries I have found on the tasting rounds.

See you online!

A sense of place

This book categorises the wines by nation of origin. This is largely to follow the manner in which retailers arrange their wines, but also because it is the country or region of origin that still most distinguishes one style of wine from another. True, wines are now commonly labelled most prominently with their constituent grape variety, but to classify all the world's wines into the small number of principal grape varieties would make for categories of an unwieldy size.

Chardonnay, Sauvignon Blanc and Pinot Grigio are overwhelmingly dominant among whites, and four grapes – Cabernet Sauvignon, Grenache, Merlot and Syrah (also called Shiraz) – account for a high proportion of red wines made worldwide.

But each area of production still – in spite of creeping globalisation – puts its own mark on its wines. Chardonnays from France remain (for the moment at least) quite distinct from those of Australia. Cabernet Sauvignon grown in a cool climate such as that of Bordeaux is a very different wine from Cabernet cultivated in the cauldron of the Barossa.

Of course there are 'styles' that winemakers worldwide seek to follow. Yellow, oaky Chardonnays of the type pioneered in South Australia are now made in South Africa, too – and in new, high-tech wineries in New Zealand and Chile, Spain and Italy. But the variety is still wide. Even though the 'upfront' high-alcohol wines of the New World have grabbed so much of the market, France continues to make the elegant wines it has always made in its classic regions. Germany still produces racy, delicate Rieslings, and the distinctive zones of Italy, Portugal and Spain make ever more characterful wines from indigenous grapes, as opposed to imported global varieties.

Among less expensive wines, the theme is, admittedly, very much a varietal one. The main selling point for most 'everyday' wines is the grape of origin rather than the country of origin. It makes sense, because the characteristics of various grape varieties do a great deal to identify taste. A bottle of white wine labelled 'Chardonnay' can reasonably be counted on to deliver that distinctive peachy or pineappley smell and soft, unctuous apple flavours. A Sauvignon Blanc should evoke gooseberries, green fruit and grassy freshness. And so on.

For all the domination of Chardonnay and Cabernet, there are plenty of other grape varieties making their presence felt. Argentina, for example, has revived the fortunes of several French and Italian varieties that had become near-extinct at home. And the grape that (in my view) can make the most exciting of white wines, the Riesling, is now doing great things in the southern hemisphere as well as at home in Germany.

Among the current market trends, the rise of rosé continues apace. Now accounting for one out of every eight bottles of still wine sold, the choice of pink brands has simply exploded. I have certainly found a greater number of interesting pinks than might have been imagined a few years ago, but there are still plenty of dull ones with suspiciously high levels of residual sugar, so choose carefully.

Rosé wines are supposed to be made from black-skinned grapes. After the crush, the skins are left in contact with the juice for long enough to impart a pleasing colour, and maybe some flavour with it, and the liquids and solids are then separated before the winemaking process continues as it would for white wine.

Some rosés are made merely by blending red and white wines together. Oddly enough, this is how all (bar one or two) pink champagnes are made, as permitted under the local appellation rules. But under prevailing regulations in Europe, the practice is otherwise forbidden. Elsewhere in the world, where winemaking is very much less strictly standardised, blending is no doubt common enough.

It is, I know, a perpetual source of anguish to winemakers in tightly regulated European nations that they have to compete in important markets like Britain with producers in Australia, the Americas and South Africa who can make and label their wines just as they please. Vineyard irrigation, the use of oak chips, and the blending in of wines from other continents are all permitted in the New World and eschewed in the Old.

But would we have it any other way? No winemaker I have met in Bordeaux or Barolo, Bernkastel or Rias Baixas seriously wants to abandon the methods and conventions that make their products unique – even with an eye on creating a global brand. And in this present difficult economic climate for wine drinkers (and winemakers) worldwide, this assurance of enduring diversity is a comfort indeed.

Spot the grape

The character of most wines is defined largely by the grape variety, and it is a source of innocent pleasure to be able to identify which variety it is without peeking at the label. Here are some of the characteristics to look for in wines from the most widely planted varieties.

White

Chardonnay: Colour from pale to straw gold. Aroma can evoke peach, pineapple, sweet apple. Flavours of sweet apple, with creaminess or toffee from oak contact.

Fiano: Italian variety said to have been cultivated from ancient Roman times in the Campania region of southern Italy. Now widely planted on the mainland and in Sicily, it makes dry but soft wines of colours ranging from pale to pure gold with aromas of honey, orchard fruit, almonds and candied apricot. Well-made examples have beautifully balanced nutty-fresh flavours. Fiano is becoming fashionable.

Pinot Grigio: In its home territory of northeast Italy, it makes wines of pale colour, and pale flavour too. What makes the wine so popular might well be its natural low acidity. Better wines are more aromatic, even smoky, and pleasingly weighty in the manner of the Pinot Gris made in Alsace – now being convincingly imitated in both Argentina and New Zealand.

Riesling: In German wines, pale colour, sharp-apple aroma, racy fruit whether dry or sweet. Faint spritz common in young wines. Petrolly hint in older wines. Australian and New Zealand Rieslings have more colour and weight, and often a minerally, limey twang.

Sauvignon Blanc: In the dry wines, pale colour with suggestions of green. Aromas of asparagus, gooseberries, nettles, seagrass. Green, grassy fruit.

Semillon: Colour can be rich yellow. Aromas of tropical fruit including pineapple and banana. Even in dry wines, hints of honey amid fresh, fruit-salad flavours.

Viognier: Intense pale-gold colour. Aroma evokes apricots, blanched almonds and fruit blossom. Flavours include candied fruits. Finish often low in acidity.

Red

Cabernet Sauvignon: Dense colour, purple in youth. Strong aroma of blackcurrants and cedar wood ('cigar box'). Flavour concentrated, often edged with tannin so it grips the mouth.

Grenache: Best known in the Côtes du Rhône, it tends to make red wines pale in colour but forceful in flavour with a wild, hedgerow-fruit style and hints of pepper.

Merlot: Dark, rich colour. Aroma of sweet black cherry. Plummy, rich, mellow fruit can be akin to Cabernet but with less tannin. May be hints of bitter chocolate.

Pinot Noir: Colour distinctly pale, browning with age. Aromas of strawberry and raspberry. Light-bodied wine with soft-fruit flavours but dry, clean finish.

Sangiovese: The grape of Chianti and now of several other Italian regions, too. Colour is fine ruby, and may be relatively light; a plummy or even pruny smell is typical, and flavours can evoke blackcurrant, raspberry and nectarine. Tannin lingers, so the wine will have a dry, nutskin-like finish.

Shiraz or **Syrah:** Intense, near-black colour. Aroma of ripe fruit, sometimes spicy. Robust, rich flavours, commonly with high alcohol, but with soft tannins. The Shiraz of Australia is typically much more substantial than the Syrah of the south of France.

Tempranillo: Colour can be pale, as in Rioja. Blackcurrant aroma, often accompanied by vanilla from oak ageing. Tobacco, even leather, evoked in flavours.

There is more about all these varieties, and many others, in 'What wine words mean' starting on page 129.

Looking for a ——— *favourite wine?* ———

If you have a favourite supermarket wine and hope to find it in this book, check the index starting on page 173.

The index is the most sensible place to start, because many of the wines I have tasted from any given supermarket, and thus entered under that chain's heading, will also be available from one or more of its rivals. I know, for example, that the top-scoring Spanish white Torres Viña Sol 2010 is sold by Asda at £5.97, but can also be found on the shelves of other retailers. I have listed it under Asda because that's where I tasted it, and to replicate this entry along with many others that are widely stocked, under all the relevant retailers, would crowd the pages with repetitions.

So, if you're interested in a branded wine you remember seeing in, say, Morrisons, don't look only in the entry for that company. Check the index for the wine, and it might just be listed under another retailer's section.

Supermarkets are raising
—the gold standard—

Last year I picked out 36 wines for perfect scores. This year it's just 26. Are standards slipping, or am I becoming more curmudgeonly? Well, maybe. But I suspect it is something less sinister. I believe I detect a significant lift in the overall quality of the wines I have been tasting. It might be connected to the fabulously ideal 2009 vintage across Europe that has produced so many of the wines featured in this edition. And I like to think it might also be the raising of skills in winemaking, especially among the great number of own-label wines here.

The effect is that there is now a growing crowd of very good wines, and the very best have to be truly outstanding to make the cut. There's a certain perverse logic to it, and there are certainly more great wines in the supermarkets than ever before. Given the economic climate, it seems a remarkable achievement to me, and these enterprising giants deserve credit for it.

Unable to resist an Olympian analogy as we gradually wind up for the great 2012 sporting blitz, I am awarding Gold this year to Tesco as the source of the most perfect scores, six in all. Silver goes to Sainsbury's with five, and Bronzes are scattered between Asda, Majestic and Morrisons with three apiece. France is way out front with ten top scores, Italy breezes in with six and Australia follows up with three.

Just a word on alcohol levels and vintages. In the descriptions of the wines, I have mentioned the alcohol by volume where it is either below 12 per cent or 14 per cent upwards. For readers to whom this information is significant, I hope this is of some help.

Nearly all the wines in the listings are made entirely or substantially from the harvest of the year stated on the label. If no vintage date is given, the wine is non-vintage or NV; it is a blend of wines made from two or more distinct harvests. This is routine for some cheaper wines, and need not matter much, except with dry white wines which, on principle, are all the better for being drunk while new and fresh. An undated dry white is not a wine to keep for any length of time.

Finally, let me plead that everything I say in this book about the wines and the retailers is based entirely on my own knowledge and understanding. Taste in all things is subjective, and more so in wine than in many other respects. I hope you will enjoy the book, and equally so, the wines.

My gold-medal wines of the year

Red wines

Cuvée Prestige Côtes du Rhône 2010	Sainsbury's	£4.54
Finest Teroldego Vigneti Delle Dolomiti 2009	Tesco	£5.99
Inycon Nero d'Avola/Frappato 2010	Waitrose	£6.69
Pasqua Passimento 2008	Co-op	£7.99
Finest Block 19 Shiraz Cabernet Sauvignon 2009	Tesco	£7.99
The Best McLaren Vale Shiraz 2006	Morrisons	£8.49
Greener Planet Red 2010 litre	Asda	£8.98
Finest Bourgogne Hautes Côtes de Nuits 2009	Tesco	£9.79
Rioja Perez Burton 2007	Marks & Spencer	£9.99
Broquel Bonarda 2009	Tesco	£10.99
Château Boutisse 2004	Majestic	£13.99
Châteauneuf du Pape Gonnet Frères 2007	Tesco	£19.99
Torre de Mastio Amarone Classico 2007	Sainsbury's	£21.99

Pink wine

Fairleigh Estate Pinot Noir Rosé 2010	Majestic	£7.49

White wines

Torres Viña Sol 2010	Asda	£5.97
Rocca Vecchia Falanghina 2010	Co-op	£5.99
Morrisons Mâcon Villages 2009	Morrisons	£6.15
Fairview La Capra Chardonnay 2010	Waitrose	£7.99
Fiano Sannio 2010	Marks & Spencer	£7.99
Finest Ken Forrester Chenin Blanc 2010	Tesco	£7.99
The Best Chablis 2009	Morrisons	£9.34
d'Arenberg The Hermit Crab Marsanne Viognier 2008	Sainsbury's	£9.99
Seifried Estate Sauvignon Blanc 2010	Sainsbury's	£9.99
Taste the Difference Pouilly Fumé 2010	Sainsbury's	£12.49
Domaine Zind Humbrecht Gewürztraminer 2009	Majestic	£14.99

Sparkling wine

Extra Special Vintage Champagne 2002	Asda	£20.17

Asda

Tasting Asda's wines at a well-organised event staged in a swish London venue is both fun and informative. The wine team, led by the redoubtable Philippa Carr MW, is skilled, articulate and dedicated to finding the best possible range on the tightest possible budget. Consequently this retail giant has a lot of good and good-value wines, and I have, as you will discover in the following pages, plenty to recommend.

Can you feel a 'but' coming? Well, yes. But this but is not about the wines. It's about the stores. When I pop into Asda hypermarkets to buy follow-up wines or simply to nose around, I find that fishing out the best buys from among the vast arrays displayed in the aisles can be a daunting task. And I am supposed to know what I'm looking for.

I shouldn't really complain. The confusion I sense on Asda's shelves embodies the case for this book. On your own, you'll struggle to find the wine you really want. Armed with *The Best Wines in the Supermarkets 2012*, you will be guided straight to the pick of the bunch.

Like my sales pitch? I make it here because I do think that Asda, of all the leading supermarkets, has the least helpful wine-shelf arrangements. And if you want the pick of the wines, you don't have the alternative of choosing them online. Unlike M&S, Tesco and Waitrose, each with whizzy wine websites offering their entire ranges (and more), Asda don't do wine for home delivery, other than the limited choice available among other groceries for local shoppers.

But let me not carp on. Asda's range of own-label wines is excellent, and compares favourably in terms of interest, quality and price with those of its competitors. They do no end of price promotions, which they insist on calling 'rollbacks', although sadly these apply almost exclusively to branded wines rather than their own range.

The numerous wines recommended here are largely from those bearing Asda's own-labels, in particular the Extra Special range. In the stores, I wish you fruitful – even happy – hunting!

RED WINES

AUSTRALIA

8 **Extra Special McLaren Vale Shiraz 2009** **£8.00**
Well-judged weight to this Tatachilla-made spicy dark and long-flavoured food wine. Roast lamb.

7 **Extra Special Coonawarra
Cabernet Sauvignon 2008** **£10.21**
Dark, ripe softie with clean edge to the plump black fruit.

7 **Asda Chilean Cabernet Sauvignon 2010** **£4.06**
Rather overtly oaked style; the fruit competes – just.

8 **Asda Malbec 2010** **£5.18**
Nicely focused savoury black-fruit flavours in this wholesome middleweight.

9 **Extra Special Malbec 2009** **£6.48**
Rich, velvety, near-black sinewy-but-juicy mouthfiller from Concha y Toro with 14% alcohol.

CHILE

9 **LFE Familia Carmenère 2009** **£7.68**
Deliciously expressive and complete rendering of the mysterious Carmenère grape is sleek, sinewy and darkly intriguing, with 14% alcohol.

8 **Mayu Sangiovese 2008** **£7.68**
The nutskin-dry finish evokes the Chianti style, and there is something of the Italian wine's bright cherry fruitiness here too, along with sunny Chilean ripeness (14% alcohol).

9 **Mayu Syrah Reserva 2007** **£9.15**
Syrah is usually called Shiraz in the New World, but this wine honours the variety's Rhône origins with its elegant, discreetly peppery and uplifting black-fruit flavours. Lovely stuff with 14% alcohol.

Red Wines

Asda — FRANCE

🍷 8 Asda Côtes du Rhône 2010 £3.83
Perfectly respectable and recognisable everyday red at a barely believable price.

🍷 8 Extra Special Beaujolais Villages 2010 £5.97
Lots of bouncy fruit in this vigorous raspberry red to serve cool.

🍷 8 Kiwi Cuvée Pinot Noir 2009 £6.16
Saucy, sweetish and easy Pinot from Corsica is nothing like the New Zealand version.

🍷 8 Extra Special Fleurie 2010 £6.48
The quality is that of a decent Beaujolais Villages, juicy and plump. 'Fleurie' in name only.

🍷 9 La Vieille Ferme 2010 £6.68
A folksy brand with chickens on the label from Rhône giant Perrin is an eager, bristling Côtes du Ventoux with easy weight and friendly spice. Ubiquitous, but irresistible.

🍷 7 Extra Special Cabernet Sauvignon 2010 £6.97
Hugely ripe Languedoc food wine has strong blackcurrant fruit slicked up with oak. Could turn out well in 2012–13.

🍷 8 The Original Malbec 2010 £7.47
The name on this Languedoc wine must be a tilt at Argentina's adoption of the Malbec grape; it's a well-aimed one, lip-smackingly savoury and dark, oak enriched and juicily ripe.

Red Wines

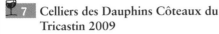

7 **Celliers des Dauphins Côteaux du Tricastin 2009** £7.98

Cheerfully abrasive midweight Rhône has warm, spicy redcurrant fruit. Made by a giant producer, watch out for this one on discount, as I see it's £5.99 at Waitrose.

8 **Château de Jau 2008** £8.17

Bold, dark and spicy Roussillon has gravitas and completeness.

8 **Les Hauts de Bonpas 2009** £8.97

Fruity-peppery Costières de Nîmes with sinewy ripeness and yet a soft, supple appeal that sneaks up on you. The price is warranted.

10 **Greener Planet 2010** £8.98

In a plastic bottle that looks standard 75cl but in fact contains a litre, this is a pure Cabernet Sauvignon of wholesome ripeness and density with heaps of vivid cassis fruit and a healthy dry finish. A remarkable product from the Languedoc at a price equating to £6.73 for a standard bottle.

9 **Extra Special Châteauneuf du Pape 2009** £14.67

This is cheap by Châteauneuf standards, and delicious into the bargain, with the levels of flavour and fruitcake complexities hoped for. Lavishly ripe and developed, with 14% alcohol.

FRANCE

RED WINES

8 **Casa Lella Nero d'Avola 2010** £5.48
Warm and spiced Sicilian with plumpness and a keen dry edge.

9 **Le Monferrine Barbera 2010** £5.98
Bustling, brambly, unserious Piedmont pasta-matcher scores 9 if you take up the permanent 3-for-£10 deal.

8 **Extra Special Montepulciano d'Abruzzo 2010** £6.98
Twice the price of bog-standard Asda Montepulciano and five times as good, this is a breezy purple lipsmacker with bouncing briar fruit, a creamy lick of richness, crunchy liveliness and nutskin-dry finish.

8 **Extra Special Valpolicella Ripasso 2009** £6.98
Velvety specialist version of Veneto's famed Valpoll includes rich Amarone wine: dark and chewy with warm, cherry ripeness.

8 **Extra Special Chianti Classico Riserva 2007** £7.14
Plenty of vanilla in this rounded-out wine after two years in oak, but there's vivacity in the black fruit too. Very proper Chianti at a fair price.

8 **Extra Special Barbera d'Asti 2009** £7.24
Safe, juicy and very ripe (14% alcohol) Piedmont red by good Araldica winery delivers a lot of briary bounce.

8 **Lobster Reef Pinot Noir 2009** £10.17
Light but lush textbook Kiwi cherry-raspberry Pinot with palpable purity of flavour.

ITALY

N. ZEALAND

RED WINES

PORTUGAL

🍷 8 Asda Portuguese Red £4.68
Non-vintage Lisbon wine has typical Portuguese clovey-minty black fruit; good with sardines.

🍷 9 Tagus Creek Shiraz Trincadeira 2010 £6.20
Particularly ripe and vivid new vintage for this familiar Lisbon brand; dark, juicy, minty-spicy fruit and 14% alcohol.

SPAIN

🍷 8 Gran Vega Garnacha 2009 £4.17
Firmly put-together Campo de Borja (Rioja neighbour) is darkly satisfying and cheap.

🍷 9 Rioja Marques del Norte 2010 £4.23
Perky, young, unoaked but authentic Rioja seems ridiculously cheap.

🍷 9 Mitico Old Vines Garnacha 2009 £6.20
Impactful, intense, savoury oaked Campo de Borja has length of flavour, 14.5% alcohol and power to match the gamiest roasts. Love it.

🍷 9 Altos de Tamaron Crianza 2007 £8.23
Pure Tempranillo from Ribera del Duero, this is sweetly, mintily ripe with good gentle abrasion of tannin and acidity; a very smooth charmer.

WHITE WINES

AUSTRALIA

8 **Extra Special Adelaide Hills Chardonnay 2009** £8.67

A welcome whiff of proving bread dough from this buttery and lavish dry food white is offset with minerality and a citrus edge.

9 **Extra Special Clare Valley Riesling 2008** £9.18

This same vintage scored 10 in last year's edition and I'm surprised to find it still on the shelf. Nose now seems a little shy, but it has the same succulent nectarine fruit and limey tang, with a hint of petrol creeping in.

CHILE

8 **Mayu Sauvignon Blanc 2010** £7.98

This one stood out from a crowd of Chilean Sauvignons for its jalapeño whiff and long, grassy, nettly fruit.

8 **Asda Vin de Pays Chardonnay 2010** £4.15

Easy-drinking Languedoc apple-fresh dry wine has a lick of toffee but is unoaked.

7 **Kiwi Cuvée Sauvignon Blanc 2010** £6.16

Artful vin de pays in no way resembles New Zealand style but is briskly enjoyable.

FRANCE

9 **Cave de Lugny Mâcon-Villages Chardonnay 2010** £6.17

Nicely ripe and mineral classic Chardonnay from ever-improving Mâconnais is long, nuanced and keen value.

8 **Château Salmonière Muscadet de Sèvre et Maine Sur Lie 2010** £6.17

Grand Loire mussel-matcher with lots of seagrass fruitiness is leesy rather than green, and easy to enjoy.

White Wines

9 **Paul Mas Marsanne 2010** £6.97
Delectably ripe, nutty and creamy, but crisp and zesty, oaked Languedoc food wine (poultry, fish, soft cheeses) from ubiquitous Jean Claude Mas.

8 **Cave de Lugny White Burgundy 2010** £7.17
Friendly mineral Chardonnay from admirable Mâconnais outfit, inexplicably costlier than the Lugny Chardonnay mentioned above.

9 **Greener Planet 2010** £8.98
Marsanne with a little Chardonnay from Minervois makes a lively but ripe and dimensional dry white of great charm, in an amazing plastic bottle of standard size but holding a litre.

8 **Ginestet Sauternes 2009 37.5cl** £9.97
Very rich and honeyed but balanced pud wine with a relatively light touch for Sauternes.

8 **Extra Special Pouilly Fumé 2010** £10.78
Pebbly-bright and grassy lush classic Loire Sauvignon worthy of the name.

FRANCE

9 **Dr L Riesling 2010** £7.18
I think this is softer than the memorable 2009, with a rush of sweet-apple fruit, a keen acidity and just 8.5% alcohol.

GERMANY

WHITE WINES

ITALY

8 Extra Special Fiano 2010 £6.13
Sweet pear aroma and long plump fruit in this gently tangy Sicilian dry wine.

9 Church Mouse Falanghina 2010 £7.23
Quaintly named Puglian dry wine is aromatic, nutty and sweet-apple ripe. A standout food wine from a grape that once made the Falernian wine of ancient Rome.

8 Extra Special Gavi 2010 £7.62
Safe but likeable, rich but racy, almondy Piedmont dry wine from dependable Araldica winery.

N. ZEALAND

8 Extra Special New Zealand Sauvignon Blanc 2010 £8.40
Big, strong gooseberry-and-asparagus number from Wither Hills winery is an emphatic mouthfiller with a saucy lick of sweetness.

S. AFRICA

8 Asda South African Chenin Blanc 2010 £3.58
I'll admit I don't expect much of Cape Chenin at this price level, but do like this one's crafty balance of tropical fruit and crisp cleanness.

SPAIN

8 Asda Moscatel de Valencia £3.73
Rich colour, honeyed grapy richness in this wicked stickie with 15% alcohol. Serve very cold, just for fun.

10 Torres Viña Sol 2010 £5.97
This enduring and inspired branded wine, launched 50 years ago, is on top form. Dry and zesty, it has a wild, grassy aroma and a crispness that summons up Cox's apples, along with sherbet and lemon. From Parellada grapes, better known in cava, and just 11.5% alcohol.

WHITE WINES

SPAIN

🍷 **8** **Villa Ludy Albariño 2010** £7.64
Yeasty, faintly oxidative and intriguing dry, long-flavoured food wine from Rias Baixas.

SPARKLING WINES

FRANCE

🍷 **10** **Extra Special Vintage Champagne 2002** £20.17
This is the third successive edition in which this miraculous champagne has featured. It is clearly a much slower seller than it deserves to be and gets more gloriously toasty-brioche rich and mellow with each year.

SPAIN

🍷 **9** **Asda Cava Semi Sec** £4.49
Manageably sweet and convincingly fresh, this is a sort of Catalan Asti Spumante, though very much more interesting and 13% alcohol; the price is amazing.

🍷 **8** **Extra Special Vintage Cava 2009** £9.98
Apples and raisins on the nose of this lively Codorniu-made wine translate into full, satisfying fruit flavours.

Booths

This 26-branch supermarket chain based in the northwest of England is much-respected locally for its high standards in all kinds of groceries. The wines (and real ales and ciders) have become well-known to a wider geographical audience thanks to a formidable website, **www.everywine.co.uk**, through which the 600-strong range on shelf in the stores can be ordered for home delivery, in any mix you like.

There is a clue in the name of the website to its wider function. As well as Booths' own range, you can also choose from about 37,000 other wines, all available for delivery by the case. It is an amazing service, though I have never really understood why a Lancastrian grocer should have diversified in a direction such as this.

The following pages deal exclusively with the wines you will find in Booths supermarkets if you are fortunate enough to be in the region. It's a good list, although in the last couple of years I have detected some diminution of choice. Some of my own perennial favourites, which I've featured for many years, such as the superb real red Medici Lambrusco and the great-value champagnes of H Blin, have been deleted in the last year.

But there is still a grand selection at sensible prices. The website is easy to operate. To order mixed wines from the store list, click on the 'mix your own case' icon. The delivery charge is £5.95. And if online ordering is too scary, there's a free phone number for you to place your order with a human being: 0800 072 0011.

Booths

RED WINES

8 **Peter Lehmann Clancy's Red 2008** £8.19
Formidable Barossa blend of Shiraz, Cabernet Sauvignon and Merlot is 14.5% alcohol but as artfully weighted as ever with its plummy depths and warm spice.

8 **St Hallet Gamekeeper's Reserve 2009** £8.29
Big Barossa beauty is largely Shiraz with some Touriga Nacional, and I swear the latter contributes the alluring porty whiff that leads into this lush and well-balanced bargain.

AUSTRALIA

9 **Réserve des Hospitaliers Côtes du Rhône Villages 2007** £8.15
Exceptional ripe and spicy Cairanne red from a vintage now in its prime, and running out fast.

9 **Morgon Domaine de Gaget Côte de Py 2009** £10.35
Rare and rarely delicious Beaujolais *cru* in the best vintage for 30 years is gloriously juicy, with burgundian gravitas in weight and structure. It will surely evolve.

FRANCE

8 **Adria Vini Rapido Rosso 2009** £4.95
Cheerfully named Campania red makes a happy marriage of brambly vigour and earthy spice from a blend of Aglianico and Sangiovese grapes.

ITALY

8 **Capcanes Mas Collet 2007** £8.29
Solid perennial from Catalan DO of Monsant is delectably dense and savoury, and benefiting from bottle age.

SPAIN

WHITE WINES

FRANCE

8 **Baron de Badassière Picpoul de Pinet 2010 £6.99**
Nice bold example of this Mediterranean shellfish-matcher has orchard perfumes and crisp citrus edge to the flavour.

8 **Seigneurs de Monbazillac 2006 50cl   £7.09**
Honeyed stickie of sinfully mellow charm from dependable Bordeaux firm Yvon Mau is a lovely elevenses wine. Finishes tighter and cleaner than other Monbazillacs I can think of.

8 **Cave de Turckheim Alsace Pinot Blanc
2009   £7.29**
You hardly ever see Pinot Blanc among the Alsace offerings in the supermarkets, so this is a find: fresh and appley but smoky and aromatic too. A fine mineral food wine.

8 **Josmeyer La Kottabe Riesling 2009   £17.49**
You don't see much of this sort of wine in supermarkets: it's an exotic, aromatic, classic dry Riesling from one of the top estates in Alsace. Enthusiasts of the style can invest with confidence.

GERMANY

9 **Dr L Riesling 2009   £7.29**
Apple-crisp, mineral and thrillingly racy 8.5% alcohol Moselle by estimable Ernie Loosen.

9 **Villa Wolf Pinot Gris 2009   £7.29**
Smartly packaged in a burgundy-type bottle, this smoky-savoury but briskly fresh dry wine from the Rheinpfalz by ingenious Ernest Loosen is close to the top of the world Pinot Grigio scale.

WHITE WINES

N. ZEALAND

🍷 8 **Villa Maria Private Bin
Sauvignon Blanc 2011** £10.15
Excitingly crisp gooseberry explosion of fruit in this cerebral nettly-fresh Kiwi megabrand. Have seen it cheaper elsewhere.

S. AFRICA

🍷 9 **Jordan Chardonnay 2009** £11.39
I don't mind admitting that this is one of my favourite Chardonnays worldwide. It's a rich, oaked Stellenbosch wine of epic ripeness, but has a relaxed naturalness to the fruit-freshness balance that leaves me in awe.

SPAIN

🍷 8 **Marques de Riscal Verdejo Rueda 2009** £7.29
Lush, grassy, super-Sauvignon-style dry white from a great Rioja name in esteemed Rueda.

🍷 8 **Viña Esmeralda 2009** £7.99
Exotic, grapy but stimulatingly refreshing dry white from Catalan dynasty Torres is a great standby as an aperitif and fish-matcher. The 2010 is well up to standard too.

Co-op

I am pleased to report that there are 45 wines from the Co-op recommended in this new edition. But there's a caveat: only a few of these will be found in the dinky convenience stores that account for the greater part of this retail giant's nationwide 3,000-branch network. A handful of the wines are available in the mere 300 outlets dubbed Fine Wine Stores. For a decent choice, you need to shop in what the Co-op calls its market town stores, or the rather scarcer superstores.

All that said, the Co-op is most emphatically on an upward curve. Not only are the shops more numerous – 100 new grocery outlets are opening every year – but they look smarter than ever and have unique attractions. It is no idle boast to proclaim 'We are the only retailer to sell food grown on our own farms, and our farming business is the largest in the UK.'

This enterprise has now been extended to wine, with the planting of the Co-op's first vineyard in Britain at Down Ampney in Gloucestershire. If all goes well, the first vintage to appear under the Co-op's Grown By Us label will appear in 2014. Watch this space.

In the meantime, there are some nifty new additions to the list this year, including two top-scoring wines from Italy and a little selection from the Fine Wine range that leaves me unhesitating in my answer to the incredulous question, 'Would you buy a £25 Meursault from the Co-op?' Yes, indeed.

The skills the Co-op buyers deploy to source their dependable everyday wine range – including the widest selection of Fairtrade labels to be found anywhere – have been diverted to extremely good effect in picking out these few de luxe wines. If you have a suitably enormous Co-op handy, you can invest with confidence.

RED WINES

ARGENTINA

9 **Finca Mirador Shiraz 2009** £6.49
Deep purple and muscular, darkly juicy and seductively oaked blackberry monster with 14% alcohol and a lot of charm.

8 **Spinsanti Cabernet Sauvignon
Reserva 2010** £6.99
Straight but not Spartan pure-blackcurrant oaked Mendoza meat-matcher has a lick of richness at the finish as well as gently gripping tannin and 14.5% alcohol.

AUSTRALIA

8 **The Lioness Shiraz 2008** £9.99
A very dark wine in every sense, this has tinglingly grippy ripeness (14.5% alcohol) managed by creamy oak and dense spiced fruit. Serious stuff.

8 **The Lodge Hill Shiraz 2009** £9.99
'Spice and coal', it says in my note; it's very darkly ripe (14.5% alcohol), but not burnt in flavour, and nicely balanced.

9 **Dead Letter Office Shiraz 2007** £11.99
In Co-op superstores only, but I must mention this cryptic McLaren Vale heavyweight; briar-vegetal nose full of dark promise leads to juicy, almost caramelly rich fruit – it's huge (15% alcohol) and superbly balanced.

CHILE

8 **Santa Rita 120 Carmenère 2010** £6.99
This old friend is startlingly concentrated and minty with long, mulberry-evoking fruit.

RED WINES

9 **Château Sainte Mathe 2007**   £6.99
Fruit and spice are nicely married in this mature and rounded Languedoc class act.

9 **Domaine Sainte Eugénie Corbières 2008**   £6.99
Garrigue flavours in this dark, robust Mediterranean winter red with the spice and tannin nicely rounded out into a rich texture.

8 **La Métropole Red 2010**   £6.99
The shocking purple colour of this Roussillon red goes with the gaudy, Goulue-style label, and the wine is joyfully juicy, just short of jammy.

7 **Mâcon Rouge Les Epillets 2010**   £6.99
From the Gamay grape of Beaujolais fame, but with slick Mâcon character, a light, charming red to drink cool.

9 **Perrin Nature Côtes du Rhône 2009**   £8.99
Its rather light, raw colour belies the heft of this grippingly good, oaked, spicy red from a great vintage now coming round very nicely.

8 **Moramari Salice Salentino 2009**   £5.49
Self-effacingly packaged Puglian Negroamaro is a pleasingly pungent and intense oaked spicy-food red of real charm, and good value.

FRANCE

ITALY

RED WINES

10 **Pasqua Passimento 2008** £7.99

This is a Veronese variation on the ripasso reds of Valpolicella, but with a good measure of Merlot. The result is a dense, velvety, black-cherry contrivance with 14% alcohol, coffee-and-fruitcake notes and a classic nutskin-dry finish. Very Italian, very delicious indeed. Superstores only (grrr).

8 **Soprasasso Amarone della Valpolicella 2007** £13.99

Easy-weighted, richly oaked specialty red with authentic 'bitter' (Amarone) rim and dark, dense fruit; 14% alcohol. Fine Wine outlets.

9 **Conte Dell'Unita Barolo 2006** £16.99

Fine wine for sure, this bricky-orange mature Barolo has weight, breadth and depth of rich cherry fruit and firm, defining tannin.

8 **Waipara Hills Pinot Noir 2009** £12.99

Leafy-scented Central Otago red is lively with plenty of woof (and 14% alcohol), with the hallmark Kiwi sleekness.

9 **Vergelegen Reserve Cabernet Sauvignon 2006** £13.99

Stellenbosch winery Vergelegen is a Cape icon, and this dark-hearted, mocha, black fruit and bitter-chocolate, beautifully structured maturing Cabernet lives well up to the mark. Fine Wine outlets.

ITALY

N. ZEALAND

S. AFRICA

RED WINES

SPAIN

Y 8 La Pradera Monastrell 2010   **£4.99**
Leafy whiff and clean, even crunchy red fruit in this light, young La Mancha red.

Y 8 Baron de Ley Rioja Reserva 2006   **£10.99**
Strawberry sweetness and creamy oak in this mature but still-grippy textbook Rioja.

PINK WINES

FRANCE

**Y 8 Mas de Cardeline Côtes de Provence
Rosé 2010**   **£8.99**
Pale coral colour but an assertively summer-fruit pink with a keen tangy edge.

S. AFRICA

Y 8 La Capra Pinotage Rosé 2010   **£7.50**
Smoked-salmon   colour,   strawberry   perfume   and corresponding summer soft-fruit flavours finishing fresh and dry.

SPAIN

Y 8 Baron de Ley Rioja Rosado 2010   **£6.99**
Shocking pink and strawberry-fresh dry style, with satisfying weight.

WHITE WINES

7 Rockbourne Estate Pinot Grigio 2010 £6.99
It could pass for Italian, and the better kind of Italian, too – dry, with a hint of grapefruit and smoke.

8 X&Y Sauvignon Blanc 2010 £8.99
Margaret River wine has grass and nettles galore, and lots of interest; not cheap, but it stands out from a very big crowd.

8 The Lodge Hill Riesling 2010 £9.99
Limey, very dry and minerally Clare Valley classic Aussie Riesling has the weight to match Asian dishes or poultry.

8 La Métropole Blanc 2010 £6.99
Gaudy label but a nicely balanced dry white from Roussillon with tropical fruits.

8 Louis Jadot St Aubin 2008 £14.99
In only 300 Fine Wine stores, but a big, buttery burgundy of real dimension and balance. A safe bet.

9 Meursault Premier Cru les Bouchères
Nicolas Potel 2008 £24.99
From a legendary Burgundy winemaker, this is the last vintage from his Meursault holding that was made by Nicolas Potel himself, pre-retirement. It is fabulous, worth it, and in Fine Wine stores only.

9 Devil's Rock Riesling 2010 £6.49
It looks Australian, but it's from the Rheinpfalz, and is a classic dry Riesling through and through, limey and racy, and – in this vintage – with a honeyed apple ripeness that offers a welcome clue to its noble origin.

WHITE WINES

GERMANY

🍷 **8** **Reichsgraf von Kesselstatt Riesling
Kabinett 2009**   **£9.99**
With a clear honey note, this elegant Moselle is surprisingly soft for a kabinett, but an eager and stimulating aperitif wine with just 8.5% alcohol.

HUNGARY

🍷 **8** **Seven Towers Chardonnay 2010**   **£5.25**
Sunny colour and matching mellow fruit in this crisp party wine at 11.5% alcohol.

ITALY

🍷 **8** **Moramari Fiano 2010**   **£5.49**
A great big ripe Sicilian spin on the splendid Fiano grape, with almondy richness and lively acidity.

🍷 **10** **Rocca Vecchia Falanghina 2010**   **£5.99**
Lemon-gold colour, a keen brassica whiff and long, lush and grassy distinctive fruit in this superb dry white from Puglia. Annoyingly, only in superstores, but worth the effort to get acquainted with the fascinating Falanghina grape.

N. ZEALAND

🍷 **8** **Bankhouse Sauvignon Blanc 2010**   **£6.99**
Light in weight but eagerly fresh and alive with a grassy rush.

White Wines

SOUTH AFRICA

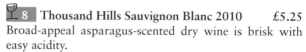 **8 Thousand Hills Sauvignon Blanc 2010** £5.25
Broad-appeal asparagus-scented dry wine is brisk with easy acidity.

8 Steenrust Chenin Blanc Barrel-Fermented 2010 £13.99
Rich in colour and texture without being sweet, this peachy de luxe white with 14% alcohol would go well with crustaceans. Fine Wine outlets.

Sparkling Wines

ITALY

8 Valdo Prosecco Treviso £8.99
Authentic 'brut' (very dry) style of the trendy Venetian fizz has lots of ripe orchard fruit, refreshing quality and 11% alcohol.

Majestic

 Majestic is a force of nature. As other high street merchants have toppled – the giant Thresher/Wine Rack chain in 2010 and, shockingly, the much-admired Oddbins in 2011 – this unique 'wine warehouse' operation continues to expand its branch network and to sell more wine. While the overall take-home wine market shrank by 3 per cent in the financial year to April 2011, Majestic's sales grew by 3.6 per cent. And while lingering economic gloom dampened demand for 'fine' wine, Majestic reported a 23.7 per cent hike in sales of bottles costing £20-plus.

How do they do it? Simple, really. Offer a wide selection of good wines at keen prices with perpetual discounts, in pleasant premises that are staffed by enthusiastic and knowledgeable young people who insist on carrying your wines to the car, which you've parked for free right outside the door.

It's brilliant. And of course, the continual promotional pricing of featured wines – buy any two bottles from Australia/Beaujolais/Chile etc., and save 20 per cent – fits in sublimely with the minimum purchase requirement of six bottles (reduced from 12 in a well-timed move just before the recession-struck Christmas of 2009).

But the real secret of Majestic's success still resides in the wines themselves. This is a range unlike any other in its breadth and depth. True, Majestic is not a supermarket. It hardly does any of the familiar brands, and of course, with a mere 160-odd branches it can afford to buy from smaller-scale producers.

Three or four times a year there is a new price list, presented like a glossy magazine, and this keeps you up to date with what's new and what's on promotion. It's well worth studying this before making a journey. Not that you need stir. You can ring up your nearest branch and order for home delivery, free for 12 bottles or more. Or you can order online if you can make the customer-registration process work – something I have, to my extreme frustration, failed to do, thus losing out on a fabulous mixed case of old German Rieslings offered exclusively online in the summer of 2011. I am still smarting.

Last word: take all the prices mentioned in the following pages with a pinch of something. Chances are that most of these wines will be available now, or shortly, at 20 per cent less than the list price if you are prepared to make the supreme sacrifice of buying two bottles.

RED WINES

ARGENTINA

🍷 **8** **Don Tiburico Bodegas Malbec Blend**
2008 £11.99
Half Malbec and the rest Bordeaux stalwarts, this is a rather slick and Médoc-like contrivance with extra Mendoza ripeness and muscle (14.5% alcohol).

🍷 **8** **Wakefield Estate Merlot 2009** £9.99
Dense, full (14.5% alcohol), clingy, ripe Clare Valley food wine (meat, mate) has positively elegant poise.

AUSTRALIA

🍷 **9** **St Hallet The Reward Cabernet Sauvignon**
2008 £10.99
Superb, minty, dark, sublimely ripe (14.5% alcohol) Barossa phenomenon is vivid, balanced and complete.

🍷 **9** **McGuigan The Shortlist**
Cabernet Sauvignon 2009 £14.99
Lovable Coonawarra pure-Cabernet fruit bomb is perfectly weighted, structured and somehow natural; aged in new oak but the richness feels as much down to the ideally ripe fruit.

CHILE

🍷 **8** **Los Vascos Cabernet Sauvignon 2010** £9.99
Tight fruit Colchagua wine from an estate owned by the Lafite Rothschilds, but this is wilder and riper than any Médoc. Fine grown-up Chilean with 14% alcohol.

🍷 **9** **Viu Manent Reserva Carmenère 2009** £9.99
Generous, minty, deep-crimson, creamy-oaked but pointy-brambly and grippy food red with concentration and 14.5% alcohol. Impressive.

RED WINES

8 **Les Galets Côtes du Rhône 2009** £6.49
Light but impactful spice and briar CdR with warm ripeness (14% alcohol) at a sensible price.

8 **Bordière Nord Syrah Grenache 2010** £6.99
Densely coloured and concentrated blackcurrant-essence Languedoc is spicy, muscular and satisfying. Try with cassoulet.

9 **Domaine Tranquillité 2008** £7.99
Bumper Languedoc red made by leading Bordeaux figure Bernard Magrez is friendly and ripe with sweet briar fruit and a spicy grip. Lovely mature wine with 14% alcohol.

8 **Beaujolais Lantignié 2009** £9.99
By Louis Jadot, a single-village (but not a *cru*) wine that's dense and spicy as well as bouncily juicy; grand Beaujolais from a great vintage.

8 **Beaujolais-Villages Chanson 2009** £9.99
Vigorously healthy mouthfiller from a respectable Burgundy negociant is not cheap, but it's jolly good and a survivor from the fast-disappearing fabled 2009 vintage.

8 **Bourgogne Pinot Noir Vieilles Vignes Nicolas Potel 2009** £11.99
Pale, cherry-ripe and slinky burgundy by one of the region's most admired producers.

9 **Chinon Clos de Danzay 2000** £11.99
Old Loire looks its age but is still very much with us: port nose, agreeable cold-tea tannin around the bold, still-brambly, bright red fruit, and fascinatingly developed. A rarity for old buffers.

RED WINES

8 **Château Peyrabon 2000** £12.99
Mature Haut-Médoc *cru bourgeois* is still ruby in colour, vigorous in its blackcurrant fruit and silky in delivery.

10 **Château Boutisse 2004** £13.99
This St Emilion *grand cru* jumped out from the crowd. Colour is dense ruby, the nose evokes the proverbial cigar box, and the fruit is pure silk, well developed, regally dark and rich, with ideal weight. From an under-rated vintage but still showing agreeable tannin grip, this is a great and wonderfully expressive bottle of claret.

9 **Louis Latour Gevrey-Chambertin 2007** £23.00
Immediately impressive, earthy, full-bodied senior burgundy with power and definition. You get what you pay for.

8 **Châteauneuf du Pape Vignoble Abeille Mont Redon 2007** £25.00
From one of the famed Rhône village's top estates in a great vintage, this is full, plump and finely spiced wine in the proper style. Price is warranted, especially with discount, if there is one.

8 **I Monili Primitivo del Tarantino 2010** £7.99
Dense carmine Puglian has sweet, dark fruit resembling cassis, but it's dry, balanced and edgy. Needs meat or pongy cheese.

8 **Avignonesi Rosso 2007** £9.99
From Merlot and Cabernet plus the Chianti grape Sangiovese, it's a kind of Tuscan claret, elegant and juicy with Italian sweet ripeness and nutskin finish.

FRANCE

ITALY

Red Wines

ITALY

9 **Vitis Divina Donato D'Angelo 2008** £9.99
Colour is browning in this terrific volcanic black-fruit
Aglianico red with spice and coffee and proper Italian
grip.

PORTUGAL

7 **Quinta de Crasto Douro Red 2009** £9.99
Bible-black table wine from a port estate has a distinct
porty whiff and chewy, black, hard-edged fruit. Like it –
but it needs time.

SPAIN

8 **Viña Eguia Rioja Crianza 2007** £7.99
One of the bargains among Majestic's 30-plus Riojas,
this has nicely defined blackcurrant top fruit and creamy
vanilla body in a satisfying, vigorous whole.

8 **Ramon Bilbao Rioja Single Vineyard 2008** £8.99
Sunny-ripe macho wine with tight tannin should round
out for years to come in its distinctly arty bottle.

Pink Wines

FRANCE

7 **Marquis de Pennautier Rosé 2010** £6.99
Well-coloured redcurranty Malbec-based Carcassonne
pink finishes big but clean; food wine.

8 **Les Signatures de Mont Tauch Rosé 2010** £7.99
A Côte de Provence pink from the ubiquitous Languedoc
co-op of Mont Tauch is pale and floral with crisp red fruit
and elegant freshness; a seafood wine.

8 **Château Pigoudet La Chapelle Rosé 2010** £8.99
The palest salmon colour but a lot of firm, red-fruit
juiciness from the Syrah grapes in this big-flavoured, dry
Provence pink. Seafood match.

PINK WINES

8 **Domaine Begude Pinot Rosé 2010**   £8.99
Coral-coloured, zingy Vin de Pays d'Oc has strawberry-raspberry juiciness and 11.5% alcohol.

8 **Berne Grande Récolte Rosé 2010**   £9.99
Onion-skin Provence pink has flowery perfume and lots of squishy soft summer fruit with a sweet centre, but it resolves into a cunningly contrived freshness and dryness.

8 **Château de Pampelonne Rosé 2010**   £10.99
It's not just the smart architectural label that warrants the price of this St Tropez salmon-pink de luxe model; fine summer-fruit perfume with an orange twist and long, fleshy fruit finishing crisply clean.

8 **AIX Rosé 2010 1.5 litres**   £19.99
Party-centrepiece magnum bottle looks great and the contents don't disappoint: pale salmon colour, defined red-fruit flavours, fresh with a discreet tinge of party sweetness.

7 **Allegrini Bardolino Chiaretto 2010**   £7.99
Coral colour, cherry whiff, a signature light, dry pink from Lake Garda.

10 **Fairleigh Estate Pinot Noir Rosé 2010**   £7.49
Interesting onion-skin colour draws you into this aboundingly fruity and fresh Marlborough pink that contrives emphatically to express the cherry-raspberry juiciness of the Pinot and to do it in the bright, crisp manifestation of a true rosé wine. Just 11% alcohol, and very fairly priced.

FRANCE

ITALY

NEW ZEALAND

Pink Wines

8 **Muga Rioja Rosado 2010** £9.99

Bright magenta refresher has raspberry-like fruit and an appreciable lemon edge: tapas wine.

SPAIN

White Wines

9 **McGuigan The Shortlist Chardonnay 2010** £14.99

Amazing quality from this Majestic 'parcel': gold, with big, inviting, sweet-apple nose, lavish oak-fermented rich fruit with trim acidity; unreconstructed luxury, but elegantly weighted.

8 **McGuigan The Shortlist Riesling 2005** £14.99

Yellow with petrol entry and limey finish, a fascinating mature dry white from the Eden Valley.

AUSTRALIA

8 **Viu Manent Reserva Viognier 2010** £9.99

Nicely controlled sweetness in this opulent, ripe (14.5% alcohol), tropical-fruit Colchagua wine.

CHILE

9 **La Grille Touraine Sauvignon Blanc 2010** £6.99

Consistent Loire twangy-grassy dry white of great appeal, this is as sunny and fresh – and good value – as ever.

9 **Vignobles des Aubas Colombard Gros Manseng 2010** £6.99

Artful Gascon vegetal dry but thoughtful sipping white.

8 **Domaine Les Yeuses Muscat Petit Grain 2010** £7.99

Dry but deliciously grapy too, this Languedoc aperitif white is a crowd-pleaser.

FRANCE

WHITE WINES

7 **Picpoul de Pinet Prestige Domaine
Guillaume Cabrol 2010**   £7.99
Light and briny refresher from the hot hills behind the
Mediterranean resort of Sète.

8 **Sancerre Les Baudrières 2010**   £10.99
Fine, pebbly style in this classic Loire Sauvignon with
fresh, long, lush fruit and clean edge.

8 **Mâcon Fuissé Domaine Thibert
Père et Fils 2009**   £11.99
Racy burgundy from a ripe vintage has richness and
minerality in fine balance.

9 **Trimach Gewürztraminer 2008**   £12.99
If supermarket Alsace Gewürz palls a bit, try the real
thing in the shape of this spiffing balanced white-fruit and
lychee heavyweight (14% alcohol) with rich complexity,
but freshness too.

10 **Domaine Zind Humbrecht
Gewürztraminer 2009**   £14.99
I can't help it – I must give 10 to this perfect Alsace. It is
the colour of Sauternes, has a tropical-fruit-basket nose
and matching fruit, and yet is as faultlessly fresh and dry-
finishing as it is exotic and complex; 14% alcohol. The
definitive Alsace Gewürz.

8 **Marsannay Louis Jadot 2009**   £17.99
Lavish and long prestige (and pricy) burgundy is creamily
oaked but also stony-fresh.

WHITE WINES

FRANCE

8 **Corton Charlemagne Louis Latour 2007** £55.00
Top-of-the-heap burgundy is yellow, richly ripe (14% alcohol), complete and balanced. A safe buy for that very special occasion.

GERMANY

9 **Ayler Kupp Riesling Margarethenhof Kabinett 2009** £8.99
Racy but honeyed, young and exhilarating Moselle with just 8% alcohol. Lovely now, it will go on for years.

8 **Prinz Von Hessen Riesling Kabinett Trocke 2008** £9.99
Quite an austere style with 11.5% alcohol, this is lemony-tangy, a true sharpener.

HUNGARY

8 **Royal Tokaji Dry Furmint 2008** £9.99
Gold-coloured exotic dry wine has cabbages and honeysuckle amid its fascinating spectrum of flavours; 14% alcohol.

ITALY

8 **Ponte del Diavolo Pinot Bianco 2010** £8.74
Aromatic and intriguing vegetal Pinot Bianco from Friuli is a rare treat, bright and fresh and delightfully distinctive.

9 **Falanghina Terredora 2010** £9.99
Heaps of ripe autumn fruit in this long, lush Campania wine from versatile local Falanghina grape.

8 **Stella Alpina Pinot Grigio 2010** £9.99
From the Alto Adige, a defined, edgy and smoky PG of refreshing character.

WHITE WINES

ITALY

9 **Tiefenbrunner Castel Turmhof**
Gewürztraminer 2009 **£15.99**
Spectacular lemon-gold Alsace-style Alto Adige wine
has huge inviting lychee aroma and deep, exotic flavours
embracing rosehip, brassica, passion fruit and more
lychee, with 14.5% alcohol. Drink alone or with foie
gras, even with expensive Asian dishes.

NEW ZEALAND

9 **Fairleigh Estate Sauvignon Blanc 2010** **£7.99**
Perennial Marlborough bargain has asparagus, seagrass,
nettles, the lot. No end of interest and cheap by Kiwi
standards, especially on perpetual discount.

8 **Main Divide Riesling 2009** **£12.49**
Yellow, petrolly, long and tropical, this limey-edged
mineral dry white is extraordinarily likeable; 11.5%
alcohol.

8 **Isabel Estate Sauvignon Blanc 2010** **£16.99**
A personal favourite, Isabel has a pure, linear directness
of fruit that sets it apart from the rest; so expressive, but
regrettably so expensive these days too.

8 **Peregrine Pinot Gris 2010** **£22.00**
Speciality Central Otago wine is super-ripe (14% alcohol)
and exotic with smoky-spicy nuances, rather like an
Alsace vendange tardive.

PORTUGAL

8 **Quinta de Azevedo Vinho Verde 2010** **£6.99**
Dry, even stony, 'green' wine has just 11.5% alcohol but
plenty of keen white fruit.

White Wines

SPAIN

9 **Vinas del Vero Gewürztraminer 2009** £7.99
Long-lost friend from Somontano tastes better than ever:
rose perfume and lush lychee fruit in a ripe but very fresh
package.

7 **Rioja Blanco Muga 2010** £10.99
Modern-style brisk and dry wine with discreet oak.

SPARKLING WINES

8 **Gratien & Meyer Saumur Blanc Brut** £8.99
Soft mousse, friendly fruit with a tangy lemon finish from
the Loire.

9 **Heidsieck Gold Top 2005** £20.00
Easy, mellow, commercial vintage champagne at a
perplexingly low price, this is a rare bargain; there's
nothing the matter with it.

8 **Champagne Barons de Rothschild** £39.00
Brut non-vintage at a huge price from the Lafite
Rothschilds; it clubs you into submission with its creamy-
brioche Chardonnay-dominated long-aged flavour. It's
delish, and at a fiftieth of the price of a nice bottle of
Château Lafite, a bit of a bargain, I suppose.

9 **Veuve Clicquot Vintage 2002** £40.00
I've had more than one taste of this fabulous fizz, and
it has put me in mind of sitting in the sun just outside a
patissier's window under a rose arbour sipping the most
piquantly refreshing and thoughtful sparkling wine ever
invented. Nuff said?

8 **Prosecco La Marca Treviso Extra Dry** £7.99
Dry rather than extra dry, with likeable orchard fruit, a
persistent fizz and 11% alcohol.

FRANCE

ITALY

——Marks & Spencer——

Italy and Spain are the strong suits in M&S's flush of new wines this year. I am crazy about the whites from the Campania region of southern Italy, made by an outfit called Cantine La Guardiense, a previously long-term supplier to Marks that went off the boil five years ago, obliging Italian and Spanish buyer Jo Ahearne MW to look elsewhere. This year she decided to give them another try: 'So one rain-drenched day I turned up at the cantine and bing! – the light went on. In those five years they've contracted the great Dr Ricardo Cotterella to direct their winemaking with his team, and the difference is monumental – purity and focus at each level.'

I love stories like this. M&S might be a huge, lumbering retailer, but that doesn't mean its buyers don't go to a lot of trouble when it comes to fishing out special wines at every price level. And Dr Cotterella's fabulous dry whites Fiano Sannio 2010 and Greco Sannio 2010 are, believe me, very special wines indeed.

There are so many delicious, individualistic, indeed unique wines at every point in the M&S range that I am confident there are many more such happy tales to tell. Certainly the new Spanish reds Ms Ahearne has found on her Iberian itinerary (it rained there, too) are real discoveries: the Majorcan Macià Batle 2010 is a gem, and the mature, mysteriously named Rioja Perez Burton 2007 is my Rioja of the year.

And so on, around the winemaking world. M&S wines are at an all-time peak for quality and choice, and for all the whispers that M&S food is rather expensive, I can find no grounds for saying any such thing about the wines. Prices are resolutely fair, and there are plenty of discounts on offer too. There are occasional '25 per cent off everything' promotions in the stores, and these seem to be even more frequent online.

The website is great because it's simple and easy to order from. You have to order by the whole case, though these are mostly six-bottle size. By no means all the wines in the stores are featured, but there are a good many on the web you won't find in the stores.

RED WINES

ARGENTINA

8 Fragoso Merlot 2010 £6.49
Best vintage I can recall of this M&S stalwart. A very plausible dense bramble-and-cherry glugger.

8 Balbi Shiraz Viognier 2010 £6.99
Grippy, spicy midweight with a real gush of redcurranty fruit and a surprise lemon twang at the finish.

AUSTRALIA

7 Burra Brook Cabernet Sauvignon 2010 £6.99
Healthy, brambly young wine from Yalumba showing signs it might round out well with time.

7 Tasmanian Pinot Noir 2009 £9.99
Simple pure and bright cherry-fruit Pinot with a nice twist of citrus at the edge.

9 Ebenezer & Seppeltsfield Shiraz 2009 £11.99
Colour is just about black, and I swear I found pomegranate on the nose; huge warm and spicy fruit and 14.5% alcohol, but by no means galumphing.

CHILE

**8 Canelo Cabernet Sauvignon
Carmenère 2009** £6.99
Purple tooth-coater has bright blackcurrant top notes, eager acidity and an insinuating toffee centre to the fruit. A Fairtrade wine (Los Robles) that really works.

8 Los Nucos Carmenère Shiraz 2010 £7.49
Bright purple wine is treacly but not unpleasantly sweet; a healthy, meat-eater's spicy red that grows on you.

8 Tobiano Pinot Noir 2008 £19.00
Pale, delicate but rich burgundy-style mature de luxe red with 14.5% alcohol and a very silky appeal.

9 Château Gillet 2009 £5.99
Textbook claret from the Bordeaux vintage of the century is developed, bursting with black fruit and noticeably pure in its rush of flavours. Seems very cheap.

8 Réserve de la Saurine Rouge 2010 £5.99
Beaujolais-like Rhône refresher is brisk and sunny.

9 Beaujolais 2009 £6.49
'Everyday' Beaujolais from Paul Sapin is juicy, crunchy, generously coloured and ripe. Seek it out while the miracle '09 vintage lasts.

8 Côtes du Rhône Villages St Maurice 2009 £6.99
Plush and spicy ripe (14% alcohol) CdR from a legendary vintage that will soon run out.

7 Château La Roseraie Dumont 2009 £7.99
Purple-black unyielding young St Emilion satellite claret will very likely be terrific in two or three years, if you can wait; 14% alcohol.

9 Mâcon Rouge 2009 £7.99
Revealing burgundy made from Gamay (Beaujolais) grapes but with burgundian gravitas as well as Beaujolais bounce. Generously ripe and long raspberry fruit.

9 Saint Aubin Les Argillers Rouge 2007 £17.00
So pale it could be dark rosé, this is nevertheless a deeply de luxe nuts-and-cherries burgundy of real poise; elegant and ripe.

RED WINES

FRANCE

♆ 8 Château Desmirail 2006 £34.00
Margaux *grand cru classé* is classic claret, nose to tail
with authentic cigar-box aroma, robust but silky fruit and
lingering tannins. Needs time, but a safe bet.

ITALY

♆ 8 Rosso di Puglia 2010 £4.99
Simple ripe and raspy Negroamaro to match sticky pasta.

♆ 8 Negroamaro 2010 £5.99
From Salento in Puglia, this vigorous hedgerow-fruit red
has dark-chocolate depths and 14% alcohol.

♆ 8 Chianti 2009 £6.99
An all-Sangiovese wine that's light in colour but not
in weight, it tastes young, bristling and very much like
Chianti.

♆ 9 Nebbiolo d'Alba 2007 £7.99
Colour turning chestnut and a nice pruny-spirity silkiness
in this off-piste Barolo make it a very convincing pastiche.
Decant it and you'll fool everybody.

♆ 8 Sovrano Chianti Riserva 2007 £7.99
Quite brown in colour with coffee notes, this smart-
looking bottle is agreeably mature. Drink soon.

♆ 8 Chianti Classico Torre Gena 2007 £9.99
Mature, powerful, assertive black-fruit food red with a
textbook clean finish. Needs meat.

♆ 9 Villa Magna Primitivo di Manduria 2008 £9.99
Nicely packaged southern heavyweight (14% alcohol) is
dark with liquorice twang and tarry depths, but juicily
fruity besides. Lush red for roast meat.

RED WINES

ITALY

9 **Renato Ratti Nebbiolo 2008** £12.99
Truffles and sweet black cherries on the nose of this endearingly named ageing superstar with lovely weight (14% alcohol) and silky but grippy texture; saucy lick of butterscotch in the aftertaste.

SOUTH AFRICA

9 **Dolphin Bay Shiraz 2010** £4.99
Good, cheap Cape wines are elusive, so a warm welcome to this peppery and nicely weighted ripe food red.

8 **Crows Fountain Shiraz Merlot
Pinotage 2009** £7.99
Multiple mélange works well in the round, with the 19% Pinotage contributing most of the interest.

SPAIN

8 **Vino de la Tierra de Extremadura 2010** £5.99
Friendly barbecue red from Tempranillo has spice and blackurrant – and 14% alcohol.

8 **Rioja Bodega Age 2009** £6.99
Genteel but lively unoaked cassis red with easy weight.

8 **Val de Pedron Monastrell 2010** £7.99
Pleasantly prickly, oaked, sinewy, young dark-hearted red has marked definition of flavour.

9 **Macià Batle Tinto Mallorca 2010** £9.99
Great to find a wine from Majorca – most of them are guzzled by visitors to the holiday island. It has a pleasantly abrasive gamey-herbaceous red fruit and lots of interest.

RED WINES

SPAIN

9 **Mencia Bierzo Escondite Perfecto 2009** £9.99
Dark maroon, exceptionally rich black-fruit, boldly intense, very Spanish red by admired Martin Codax in emerging Bierzo region, with 14% alcohol.

10 **Rioja Perez Burton 2007** £9.99
Mature, creamy luxury Rioja with controlled oak and rich, muscular fruit is simply scrumptious; I can find no fault with it – even the price fits.

USA

9 **Freedom Ridge Monterey Shiraz 2009** £7.99
Remarkable dense purple Californian blockbuster (14.5% alcohol) has velvet raspberry-concentrate richness but elegant balance too. With new-oak treatment and evident longevity it seems cheap at the price.

8 **Schug Sonoma Coast Pinot Noir 2009** £14.99
Silky and earthy natural-tasting Californian has nuanced appeal at a price.

PINK WINES

FRANCE

9 **Réserve de la Saurine Rosé 2010** £6.49
Pale coral Rhône is a standout pink with expressive summer-fruit flavours, long and elegant palate. Grown-up rosé and good value.

SPAIN

8 **Valdepomares Rioja Rosado 2010** £5.99
Shocking pink, frankly fruity Tempranillo from Rioja is dry, juicy and fresh.

8 **Navarra Rosado 2010** £6.99
Magenta colour and lots of vibrant redcurrant fruit.

WHITE WINES

ARGENTINA

7 **La Finca Pinot Grigio 2010** £6.49
Crowd-pleaser with sweet, peary whiff and soft orchard fruit.

8 **Balbi Pinot Grigio 2010** £6.99
Brassica nose, peachy flavours, long but trim finish – a pleasant surprise.

8 **Altos del Condor Sauvignon Gris 2010** £7.99
Big (14% alcohol) Mendoza dry grassy refresher in Sauvignon Blanc style is long and gently tangy.

CHILE

8 **Los Nucos Chardonnay Viognier 2010** £5.49
Budget fruit-salad in a glass shows both crispness and satisfying mellowness.

9 **PX Elqui 2010** £5.49
Pedro Ximénez grapes from parched Elqui Valley make a remarkably fresh and full dry wine with long, healthy, leafy flavours.

8 **Casa Leona Chardonnay 2010** £6.49
M&S perennial unoaked but creamily leesy sweet-apple straight Chardonnay.

FRANCE

7 **Vin de Pays du Gers 2010** £4.29
Fresh, just a little green, austerity dry white from admirable Plaimont co-op.

8 **Muscadet 2010** £5.49
Mild-mannered but agreeably briny and fruity straight moules wine. Cheap.

WHITE WINES

FRANCE

🍷 8 **White Burgundy 2010**   £7.99
Unoaked but substantial Mâconnais Chardonnay is flintily fresh and recognisable.

🍷 8 **Chablis Domaine Pierre de Préhy 2008**   £12.99
Creamy but unoaked maturing Chablis of mineral purity and instant appeal by ingenious producer Brocard.

🍷 8 **Falanghina Beneventano 2010**   £5.49
Fresh, bordering on spritzy, Campania summer white is bright and uplifting.

🍷 8 **Piemonte Cortese 2010**   £5.49
Vigorous stonily-fresh but almondy-creamy dry style from reliable Araldica winery near Asti.

ITALY

🍷 10 **Fiano Sannio 2010**   £7.99
Fabulously distinctive dry white from the Campania is lush with autumn orchard fruit enriched with hazelnut creaminess and yet vivid with spring freshness. Revived Fiano grape (a favourite of ancient Romans) is the variety to follow.

🍷 9 **Greco Sannio 2010**   £9.99
Look at the colour, gold shot with green, and contemplate the long, herbaceous fresh flavours. A remarkable Campania wine from a rare grape imported millennia ago by Greeks.

WHITE WINES

NEW ZEALAND

🍷 9 **Kaituna Hills Sauvignon Blanc 2010**   £8.99
While other Kiwi Sauvignons lose their edge, this perennial from giant Montana retains real zest and grassy tang, with lots of asparagus further along in the flavour.

🍷 8 **Marlborough Sauvignon Blanc 2010**   £8.99
Sweeter than the Kaituna above, but perky, too – in its own way.

🍷 9 **Lone Range Heretaunga Chardonnay 2009** £9.99
From vaunted Craggy Range in Hawkes Bay, a well-coloured weighty wine with long, ripe, peachy-oaked flavours; a luxury item.

SOUTH AFRICA

🍷 8 **Rockridge Chardonnay 2010**   £6.99
Green nose, yellow fruit and mineral brightness to this Robertson-region 14%-alcohol seafood-matcher.

🍷 9 **Workhorse Ken Forrester Chenin Blanc
2010**   £7.49
Classy Stellenbosch winery's dry and clean but toffee-hinting lush wine is superbly contrived.

SPAIN

🍷 8 **Valdepomares Rioja Blanca 2010**   £5.99
Modern-style unoaked Viura is a green and grassy refresher, more in the Rueda style than Rioja.

USA

🍷 8 **Freedom Ridge Monterey Chardonnay
2009**   £7.99
From a blend including new-oak-matured wine, this is lavish and long, a workable pastiche of posh white burgundy. Fun.

SPARKLING WINES

8 **Sparkling English Brut** £17.99
From Chapel Down in Kent, with extra grapes from Sussex and Essex, you get lots of lively mousse and a convincing bready richness; own-label champagne price and comparable quality.

9 **Ridgeview Marksman Brut**
Blanc de Blancs 2008 £22.00
From Chardonnay grapes grown on the Sussex Downs, an extraordinary champagne-style vintage fizz with gold colour, rich, yeasty flavours and irresistible charm.

7 **Oudinot Rosé** £25.00
Pink house champagne has fine onion-skin colour and nicely defined summer red fruit, at a price.

8 **Saint Gall Vintage Premier Cru 2004** £29.00
Long, luxurious and mellow blanc de blancs champagne warrants the price.

7 **Bluff Hill Sparkling Rosé** £9.99
Perky party-frock pink fizz from Chardonnay and Pinot Noir is strawberry ripe but very dry.

9 **Single Estate Chardonnay Cava 2009** £9.99
Made by estimable Segura Vidas, a well-coloured and attractively peachy fizz with plenty of ripe fruit and a brisk dryness.

ENGLAND

FRANCE

N. ZEALAND

SPAIN

Morrisons

Morrisons gets my Wine Olympics Gold Medal for 2012 for being the most-improved supermarket wine retailer of the year – by the proverbial mile.

In last year's edition of *Best Wines in the Supermarkets* I used this space to complain that Morrisons had not invited me to taste their wines, and that I was peeved. Well, this year I have been much cheered up, after being included in a major tasting of the new own-label ranges they have introduced as a significant part of an overall sprucing-up of the list.

I particularly enjoyed meeting the enthusiastic wine-buying team, and was lucky enough too to encounter a couple of the winemakers, over from the Continent especially for this occasion. One of them I mistook for just another of my wine-writing colleagues and absent-mindedly remarked to him that he should try the white I had just sampled. It was Morrisons The Best Chablis 2009. He at once poured himself a centimetre or two, took a sniff and beamed at me. Did I like it? 'Certainly do,' I told him. 'That's good,' he said, 'because my company (well, a co-operative to be exact) made it.' He was Marc Vachet, sales manager of the Union des Viticulteurs de Chablis, and I was very pleased indeed to meet him.

To summarise, things are looking up sharply at Morrisons. I found plenty of wines I liked very much, especially among the own-label The Best range, which I suppose could be described as mid-price, and some bargains too among the more everyday own-labels. It all amounts to a huge improvement in variety and depth, and I hope this is the beginning of a bright new dawn for this thoroughly decent supermarket's wine enterprises.

Morrisons

ARGENTINA

8 Trivento Reserve Syrah Malbec 2009 £7.99
Near-black blend makes the most of the spicy Shiraz and the dark, leathery savour of the Malbec; serious, satisfying red-meat wine with 14% alcohol.

AUSTRALIA

9 Morrisons Australian Shiraz
Cabernet Sauvignon £4.52
A familiar blend, but this one is unusual; blended from more than one vintage it has come out marvellously mellow and wholesome, with genial spice and relishable juicy dark fruit. Underpriced by a mile.

10 Morrisons The Best McLaren Vale
Australian Shiraz 2006 £8.49
From its dense, mature-looking ruby colour through the opulent, high-toned nose and into the depths of the juicy-spicy-toasty intense black fruit, this fabulous wine from Geoff Merrill is the complete experience. It's huge (14.5% alcohol) but it's poised, elegant, and uplifting – and cheap at the price.

8 Smith & Hooper Merlot 2008 £9.19
Tastebud-grappler has long, long, black super-ripe fruit with good poise and weight (though 14% alcohol).

CHILE

8 Morrisons Chilean Carmenère 2009 £7.37
A very dark and ripe centre in this long and toasty-oaked blackberry red will make it a nifty match for rare beef.

RED WINES

9 Morrisons Beaujolais 2009 £4.37
A pale purple, but this is no shrinking violet: a lively, juicy, squashed-raspberry Beaujolais from a brilliant vintage, with a tinge of white pepper; light, but bursting with life.

8 Morrisons French Cabernet Sauvignon £4.49
Healthy, clingy picnic red with grippy black fruit and juicy liveliness.

8 Morrisons Claret 2009 £4.99
Plenty of substance to this 70/30% Merlot/Cabernet mix from a marvellously ripe vintage.

8 Château Tour de Buch 2009 £6.49
Solid purple colour and 14% alcohol remind what a ripe vintage 2009 was in Bordeaux, making this clean, pure-fruit, Merlot-dominated wine memorably generous and forward.

8 Morrisons Claret Reserve £6.79
Interestingly, a non-vintage wine, 60/40% Cabernet/Merlot and unoaked in spite of the 'Reserve' tag, but this is developed and rounded as well as vigorous in its gripping blackberry way. Made by Sichel – and likeable.

8 Castelmaures Corbières 2008 £6.99
Gripping, dark and spicy Mediterraean red has a hint of silk; easy, rounded and 14% alcohol.

8 Cuvée Briot Rouge 2009 £7.95
Friendly, straight, brambly Bordeaux 70/30% Merlot/Cabernet mix from great vintage is juicy and wholesome.

FRANCE

RED WINES

8 **Morrisons Italian Chianti 2009** £5.19
I promise it does say Italian Chianti on the label, and I was charmed by the cherry perfume, grippy dark fruit with nutty richness and dry finish. Proper Italian Chianti indeed.

8 **Italia Primitivo 2010** £6.79
An engaging Puglian varietal with firm but juicy and direct black fruit; ignore discouraging minimalist label.

9 **Morrisons The Best Montepulciano d'Abruzzo 2009** £6.99
Dark, dense and juicy with long, brambly fruit and a defining dry finish, this is healthy, vigorous and very Italian.

8 **Morrisons The Best Valpolicella Ripasso 2009** £6.99
Nice fruitcake aroma off this quirky Verona wine, with dense colour and a dark, pruny-liquorice centre to the intense flavours.

9 **Trezanti Rosso 2009** £9.99
Lovely silky rounded surprise Salento (Puglia) red from Negroamaro grapes with mild oak richness, long fruit and spicy highlights.

8 **Barolo Cantine Gemma 2005** £14.49
Old wine browning nicely has an authentic, faintly spirity, cold-tea nose and warm, gently spicy cherry fruit with 14% alcohol. Sounds frightful, I realise, but good of its kind.

ITALY

RED WINES

SOUTH AFRICA

🍷 8 **Morrisons South African Shiraz 2010**   £6.39
There seems more of the Cape than of Shiraz in this tarry,
mega-ripe, liquorice-centred 14% alcohol, oaked fruit
bomb, but I liked it just the same.

🍷 8 **Morrisons The Best South African
      Pinotage 2009**   £7.39
Deep, attractively developed colour and sinewy-savoury
dark fruit in this authentic oaked Pinotage with spiky
highlights; assertive, not overweight, and 14% alcohol.

SPAIN

🍷 8 **Morrisons Viña Eneldo Rioja Crianza 2007** £7.79
Quite light in colour and weight (as plenty of Riojas are),
this still has a friendly plumpness of summer soft fruit
and a twang of citrus to balance the vanilla oak.

🍷 8 **Morrisons Rioja Reserva 2006**   £9.49
Colour is gently browning with age and the sweet creamy
oak is catching up with the soft blackcurrant fruit, but it
works smoothly and comfortingly overall.

WHITE WINES

AUSTRALIA

🍷 8 **Morrisons Australian Chardonnay**   £4.79
Non-vintage, but from the redoubtable Kingston Estate
in Riverland, this lively, unoaked, dry white delivers good
fruit and zest for the money.

CHILE

🍷 8 **Morrisons The Best Chilean Chardonnay
      2010**   £7.49
Spring greens and mango team up equably in this
substantial Casablanca dry white.

WHITE WINES

8 **Morrisons French Chardonnay** £4.15
Non-vintage Languedoc is in the 'soft, ripe apple and touch of buttery scrambled egg' style and really rather good.

8 **Morrisons Muscadet 2010** £4.29
Twangy Loire mussel-partner is briny and fresh with manageable acidity and plenty of interest at a keen price.

10 **Morrisons Mâcon Villages 2009** £6.15
The gold colour, the peachy-tropical Chardonnay aroma and the long, rich (but unoaked) fruit in this plush burgundy forbid me from giving it any less than maximum score when the price is taken into account.

9 **Morrisons Touraine Sauvignon 2010** £6.45
Crunchy brassica nose on this generic Loire grabs the attention, translating into an asparagus-anointed grassy-briny flavour of generous character.

8 **Vouvray Clos Palet 2009** £7.35
Interesting, mildly sweet Loire wine has good citrus balance to the delicate honeyed richness.

9 **Morrisons Petit Chablis 2009** £7.85
Loved this instantly recognisable, light-but-firm Chablis with its green-gold colour, flinty Chardonnay whiff and long, mineral flavours. Price is very fair for this sort of quality.

8 **Les Signatures Picpoul de Pinet 2010** £7.99
From the Mont Tauch co-op at Fitou, quite a burly Picpoul, ripe and full but with a clean, lemon balance.

WHITE WINES

10 **Morrisons The Best Chablis 2009** £9.34
From the same source as the Petit Chablis above, the
Union des Viticulteurs, this is a fuller, weightier wine with
similar charms. Pure and flinty in the proper Chablis way,
it is healthily leesy and long – and, I am told by Marc
Vachet of the Viticulteurs, will keep and improve in the
bottle for years.

7 **Morrisons The Best Sancerre 2009** £10.99
Creamy example of the Loire's smartest Sauvignon is
attractively balanced and will appeal to those who don't
like their Sancerre too green, or too expensive.

8 **Morrisons Mosel Riesling 2009** £6.69
Sweet-apple style with a well-wrought citrus edge and
8.5% alcohol.

8 **Morrisons The Best Auslese 2009** £8.49
Ripe rather than sweet Mosel Riesling has healthy appley
fruit and 8% alcohol. Stimulating aperitif wine.

8 **Morrisons Italian Pinot Grigio** £4.49
Liked this non-vintage, well-coloured, peachy-nosed
'Italian' PG with its fresh flavours and hint of the exotic.

8 **Morrisons Verdicchio Classico 2010** £4.79
In the kind of amphora-shaped bottle I had believed
extinct, a sunny example of the Marches café white with
lively, herbaceous, white-fruit charm.

9 **Morrisons Orvieto Classico 2010** £4.99
The delicate Orvieto wines of Umbria are lately out
of vogue, but here is a fine reintroduction, fresh with
almondy notes and finishing with a clean lemon tang.

WHITE WINES

Morrisons (vertical, left margin)

ITALY

🍷 8 **Morrisons The Best Gavi 2010** £7.49
Lively and long, herbaceous-blanched-hazelnut, discreetly rich, dry Piedmont wine by reliable Araldica.

NEW ZEALAND

🍷 8 **Morrisons The Best Marlborough Sauvignon Blanc 2010** £7.99
Crisp, nettly and fresh with edgy acidity, this finishes very trim.

🍷 8 **Crux Marlborough Sauvignon Blanc 2010** £10.49
Asparagus on the way in, seagrass and nettles in the glittery green fruit, and fun on the finish.

SPAIN

🍷 9 **Floralis Moscatel Oro 50cl** £8.05
Great Torres sweet wine has an autumn gold colour and a perfume as floral as the name suggests – from roses to lemon verbena. The flavour is faithful to the lush and refreshing juiciness of Muscat grapes. Honeyed, but not cloying.

SPARKLING WINES

FRANCE

🍷 8 **Morrisons Champagne Brut** £17.69
Generous, yeasty mouthfiller with lots of Pinot Meunier is good fun and good value.

Sainsbury's

With own-label wines such a dominant theme in this edition, I think it's time to give credit where it's due to the inventor of the genre. It was Sainsbury's, back in the 1970s.

Supermarket wine shelves before that time had been populated exclusively by brands such as Don Cortez and Hirondelle, whose uniform continental dullness was marginally relieved by cheery interlopers from more exotic climes. I recall, not without nostalgia, names like Red Infuriator (from Morocco) and Kanga Rouge (no prizes for guessing).

And then along came Sainsbury's Claret, and the rest. The other supermarkets followed on fast, but Sainsbury's maintained their lead by introducing a range of upmarket wines called Vintage Selection. Included were château-bottled clarets, proudly stickered as specially chosen for the honour of inclusion in this supermarket's exclusive range. Again, the other chains hastily followed suit.

By the 1980s, the traditional wine trade was beginning to take notice. In my treasured 1982 copy of *The Which? Wine Guide*, a volume dedicated almost entirely to exclusive wine merchants now long extinct, Sainsbury's was applauded by none other than Jancis Robinson for its value, 'particularly at the very bottom of the price range'. She heaped special praise on Sainsbury's red and white Bergeracs, at £1.55, which had 'delighted thousands throughout the summer of 1981'. The other supermarkets in the current Big Four – Asda, Morrisons and Tesco – got no mention in the guide at all.

And now? Its competitors have certainly caught up again, but at the 2011 tasting, I found plenty of evidence that Sainsbury's is still as resourceful as ever, and offering some cracking wines at all points along the price scale.

This is especially true of the own-label wines, from the rock-bottom-price 'House' range introduced last year as an antidote to the rigours of recession, through the consistently splendid Taste the Difference bottles, now numbering 55 different wines, to a brand new upmarket offering called the Classic Selection – grand vintages from about £20 upwards. It takes me straight back to the Vintage Selection of all those many years ago, and I wish Sainsbury's well with it.

RED WINES

AUSTRALIA

8 **Peter Lehmann Grenache Shiraz 2010** **£8.99**
A big, brown bronco from the Barossa, this is velvety with a startling contrast of lifted juicy fruit; 14.5% alcohol.

8 **The Olive Branch Grenache 2009** **£8.99**
Defined McLaren Vale red-fruit gripper has long, spicy flavours and 14.5% alcohol.

8 **d'Arenberg High Trellis**
Cabernet Sauvignon 2009 **£10.99**
I'd have thought the last thing you needed in McLaren is a high trellis, but this sleek Cabernet by no means seems over-ripened. Still purple and tannic, it shows many signs of excellence, but needs five years; 14.5% alcohol.

9 **Yering Station Shiraz Viognier 2007** **£10.99**
Slinky de luxe red with mint and creamy cassis fruit is artfully contrived with expensive new-oak ageing and the dollop of softening Viognier, but I was completely taken in. Delicious – and 14.5% alcohol.

9 **Gulf Station Pinot Noir 2010** **£11.99**
Deep-coloured Yarra Pinot is earthy and silky with a white pepper garnish to the sleek raspberry savour; long, and reassuring.

CHILE

8 **Taste the Difference Fairtrade**
Carmenère 2010 **£6.99**
Sleek and supple fruit in a firm structure with long black-fruit flavours.

RED WINES

8 **Sainsbury's House Corbières** £3.39

A roasty, not charred, centre to the big peppery flavour of this densely ripe Med red will make it a bargain winter warmer; 14% alcohol.

8 **Cité de Carcassonne L'Esprit de la Cité Merlot 2010** £4.49

Dense, blood-red cheapie has black-cherry whiff and a baked dark fruit, finishing clean; a beguiling hearty food red.

10 **Sainsbury's Cuvée Prestige Côtes du Rhône 2010** £4.54

A 'prestige' cuvée at this price? Well, yes. It's a deep purple, ripe and spicy monster with masses of healthy beetroot savouriness and satisfying depths. And it's weirdly cheap.

8 **Longue-Dog Red 2010** £5.49

Gimmicky Beziers Grenache–Syrah blend is artfully toffeeish with a raisiny middle, and somehow it all works.

7 **Domaine du Colombier Chinon 2009** £6.29

Strong Loire Cabernet Franc has green leafy edge to its grippy black fruit, and needs time.

9 **Taste the Difference Faugères 2009** £7.99

I like the pungent, baked bitterness of this remote Med AC, and this is a good one: nearly black and with a dark, chilli-chocolate heart and 14% alcohol. Needs meat, and starch.

RED WINES

FRANCE

8 Taste the Difference Languedoc Red 2010   £7.99
I wouldn't have thought Languedoc was a location sell for a £7.99 wine, but this is very good, with its big purple colour, briar nose and intense, controlled, black-fruit spicy ripeness.

7 Châteauneuf du Pape
Clos de l'Oratoire 2008   £18.99
High-toned vanilla whiff to this grand, 14.5% alcohol, prestige Rhône; it's a bit closed up, but delivers a big, fruit-basket mouthful in the proper manner. An investment for three years' time.

8 Chanson Nuits St Georges 2008   £24.99
It's a lot money for a generic Nuits, even if it's from a respectable outfit like Chanson, but you do get what you pay for: silky, ready-to-drink burgundy, expressive, long and sublimely balanced. Classic Selection.

ITALY

8 Taste the Difference Marzemino 2010   £5.99
An interesting departure: this is an indigenous light red of sub-Alpine Italy, surely unknown in Britain but pleasingly bright with violet notes and a Beaujolais-like appeal.

8 Taste the Difference Tuscan Red 2009   £5.99
Poor-man's Chianti from the correct Sangiovese/Canaiolo grapes is nicely weighted with cherry-raspberry fruit and authentic nutskin finish.

9 Taste the Difference Primitivo 2009   £6.99
Ruby going brown and with mellow fruit, it seems developed beyond its years, with notes of mocha and preserved fruits amid an elegant whole. Not the raw brute I expected at all.

RED WINES

8 **Piccini Montepulciano d'Abruzzo Riserva 2008** £9.99
Dense, browning, coffee-and-fruitcake mature oaked Adriatic red with flavours as gaudy as its Italianate label. Both earthy and silky, I like its elaborate style.

8 **Taste the Difference Barbaresco 2008** £9.99
Colour is pale cherry going brown and nose is cold tea, but this grippy, savoury dry cherry red is legit; smart name for show-offs at an unusually realistic price.

8 **La Capannuccia Chianti Rufina Riserva 2000** £14.99
Esoteric Chianti of rare maturity is going bricky orange in colour and shows piquant raspberry fruit through the smooth oaking; not yet drying out, but do not delay. Classic Selection.

10 **Torre de Mastio Amarone Classico 2007** £21.99
Gorgeous, nutty-rich, chocolate-dark but dry-finishing specialty Valpolicella evokes Christmas pud, complete with brandy butter; huge wine (15% alcohol) to sip like port with cheese. Pricy, but the best of its kind I have tasted. Classic Selection.

8 **Taste the Difference Hawkes Bay Gimblett Gravels Syrah 2009** £11.99
Dry and mineral plummy wine has genteel spiciness and a background toffee richness. Intriguing Kiwi spin on northern Rhône Syrah – quite delicious.

8 **Waipara Hills Central Otago Pinot Noir 2010** £12.99
Particularly earthy and ripe raspberry seducer to match poultry. Try it cool.

RED WINES

N. ZEALAND

 9 **Villa Maria Cellar Selection
Pinot Noir 2009** £14.99
Callow colour, but already sweetly rounded in its strawberry/raspberry-eucalypt lushness, this is perfectly poised, with 14% alcohol. Classic Selection.

PORTUGAL

8 **Flor de Nelas Seleção 2009** £7.99
A dark contrivance from port grapes grown in the Dão region, this is succulent with sweet, coconutty oak ageing, and instantly appealing.

ROMANIA

9 **Sainsbury's House Pinot Noir** £4.29
Pale but respectable colour and a Beaujolais-like scent lead into an unexpectedly tightknit raspberry Pinot fruit; substance, earthiness and intensity are all here, and the price is inexplicable.

SOUTH AFRICA

8 **Taste the Difference Fairtrade
Pinotage 2010** £7.99
Piquant example of the inimitable Pinotage has a nice definition of berry-minty flavour against the background of smooth oak; 14% alcohol.

8 **Taste the Difference Fairtrade
Cabernet Sauvignon 2010** £9.99
I'd say this is in the Bordeaux style, elegant and balanced, but with extra ripeness (and 14% alcohol). Generous mellow cassis style even so young.

8 **Bellingham The Bernard Series Syrah 2009** £10.99
Hat-black, hefty, defined Syrah with power and lifted flavours, and 14% alcohol.

RED WINES

S. AFRICA

🍷 9 **Kanonkop Kadette 2009** £10.99

Pinotage-based blend from a famed Stellenbosch estate is a strong, minty-tarry, spicy but discreet smoothie with a clingy finish and 14% alcohol. Special.

SPAIN

🍷 7 **Rio de la Vida Tempranillo Shiraz 2010** £5.99

Juvenile La Mancha juice bomb with blackberry charm.

🍷 9 **El Portico Crianza 2007** £9.99

A jump-out Rioja with unusually dense colour, sweetly ripe but gripping vanilla-creamy oaked fruit and juicy, healthy appeal.

🍷 8 **Condado de Haza Ribera del Duero 2007** £15.99

Very dense purple monster with 14% alcohol and minty-blackcurrant dark rich fruit with a lick of vanilla. Plush and serious. Classic Selection.

🍷 9 **Luis Cañas Coleccion Privada Rioja Reserva 2004** £16.99

Youthful colour gives no clue to the longevity of this hugely complex and rich, silky-oaked classic Rioja with 14.5% alcohol. Maker Luis Cañas is 82 and his wine seems similarly evergreen. Classic Selection.

PINK WINES

FRANCE

🍷 7 **Sainsbury's Côtes du Rhône Rosé** £4.99

Magenta, dry and crisp non-vintage has freshness.

S. AFRICA

🍷 8 **Sainsbury's Fairtrade Pinotage Rosé** £5.99

Deep colour and a basket of strawberries and crunchy pears for fruit.

WHITE WINES

7 **Taste the Difference Redbridge Creek Chardonnay 2010** £5.99
Affordable dry style with a bit of sweet coconut oak.

9 **Taste the Difference Hunter Valley Semillon 2006** £8.99
Lush pineapple-banana aroma and fruit in a developed wine retaining bright freshness, seductive appeal and just 10.5% alcohol.

10 **d'Arenberg The Hermit Crab Marsanne Viognier 2008** £9.99
I'm a sucker for this lemon-gold McLaren Vale classic with its rich mineral combo of luscious fruit and vital refreshment. Worth shelling out for.

8 **Taste the Difference Grüner Veltliner 2010** £7.99
Sweet-smelling but briskly dry-tasting exotic food wine has lots of vegetal interest.

8 **Castillo de Molina Sauvignon Blanc 2010** £7.99
Asparagus on the nose is emphatically carried through to the flavour in this distinctive, emphatic, crisp Chilean with length and edge.

9 **Taste the Difference Mâcon Villages 2010** £6.49
Big, classy, near-eggy southern burgundy in the plush, sunny style is unoaked, dancingly fresh and good value. Classic Chardonnay on its home ground.

WHITE WINES

8 Taste the Difference Muscadet de
Sèvre et Maine Sur Lie 2010 £6.49
Dry but not bone dry, and tangy just short of eye-watering, this is a proper Muscadet with palpable green fruit, verve and balance.

8 Elegant Frog Viognier 2010 £7.99
From ubiquitous (and elegant) Languedoc wine giant Jean Claude Mas, a nicely poised, rich-but-perky Viognier with genteel oak.

8 Taste the Difference Languedoc White 2010 £7.99
Generous, dry Mediterranean sunny wine from a classy grape blend resembles the luxurious style of hugely expensive white Hermitage.

9 Taste the Difference Petit Chablis 2010 £7.99
There's nothing small about this Chablis: it's well-coloured with just the right balance between flint and crisp-apple Chardonnay fruit and sunny spearmint and almond richness. Great value.

9 Taste the Difference Touraine
Sauvignon Blanc 2010 £7.99
Anon-sounding Loire wine is in fact excitingly zingy, nettly and fresh, well up to the standard of grander appellations.

10 Taste the Difference Pouilly Fumé 2010 £12.49
The price has lifted by 50% over the last five years, but this remains an outstanding buy with a friendly sherbet twitch in this new vintage's long, lush, grassy-asparagus fruit. A very special Sauvignon, and hugely better than its Sancerre counterpart at Sainsbury's this year.

Sainsbury's

FRANCE

WHITE WINES

FRANCE

🍷 8 **Sancerre Roc de L'Abbaye 2010** £15.99
Bristlingly fresh and lemony style to this lush, pebbly
Loire classic Sauvignon. Not cheap, but very cheering.
Classic Selection.

GERMANY

🍷 8 **Dr Loosen Gracher Himmelreich
Riesling Kabinett 2010** £11.99
Apple-juice-fresh-off-the-vine Moselle of fine mineral
character to relish now or keep for any length of time;
7.5% alcohol. Classic Selection.

ITALY

🍷 7 **Taste the Difference Verdicchio Classico
di Jesi 2010** £5.99
I was underwhelmed by Sainsbury's 2010 Italians, but
this one was OK: fresh and prickly with a sly backgroud
sweetness.

🍷 9 **Ascheri Gavi di Gavi 2010** £12.99
Rich colour and sweet almondy nose on this Classic
Selection dry white from a famed Piedmont estate;
pellucid white-fruit flavours with almondy richness.

NEW ZEALAND

🍷 8 **Wither Hills Chardonnay 2010** £9.49
I like the smoky apple style and gentle minty creaminess.

🍷 10 **Seifried Estate Sauvignon Blanc 2010** £9.99
On first contact I thought this perennial favourite might
be a bit austere in this vintage, but then it dawned that
this is what I've been missing in Kiwi Sauvignons of late.
This is flawlessly fresh, zesty, grassy and generous. Solid
gold. Also at Morrisons.

WHITE WINES

NEW ZEALAND

🍷 8 **Taste the Difference Single Block Vineyard Sauvignon Blanc 2010** £9.99

Stands out for its bold, briny grassiness on the way to a lick of rich ripeness at the edge; 14% alcohol.

🍷 8 **Cloudy Bay Sauvignon Blanc 2010** £18.99

Iconic brand that begat the Kiwi wine phenomenon lives up to the name, if not the price, with a strong asparagus whiff and corresponding lush, grassy fruit, finishing crisp rather than tangy. Classic Selection.

S. AFRICA

🍷 8 **Taste the Difference Fairtrade Chenin Blanc 2010** £7.99

Clean, wholesome, dry white from Wellington region has a likeable balance of mango fruit and citrus twang.

🍷 7 **Rio de la Vida Airén Sauvignon 2010** £5.99

Fresh, dry, party white from La Mancha is easy to like and claims to be just 8.5% alcohol.

SPAIN

🍷 9 **Spanish Steps Rueda 2010** £6.99

Lush, peachy Verdejo is perfectly balanced with grassy freshness. A bargain.

🍷 9 **Taste the Difference Albariño 2010** £7.99

Hint of gunflint on the nose of this cracking Rias Baixas dry wine; long, seagrass flavours with a keen lemon tang. A perennial classic.

Sainsbury's

SPARKLING WINES

FRANCE

9 **Sainsbury's Blanc de Noirs**
Champagne Brut £17.77
Fabled yeasty beastie mostly from Pinot Meunier is rich in colour and bready bright fruit; tastes way, way above price.

ITALY

7 **Mondelli Sparkling Rosé 2010** £8.99
Prawn pink and sweet within reason, an Asti-style foamer with cheery strawberry flavour and 7.5% alcohol.

7 **Taste the Difference Prosecco Conegliano**
2010 £9.99
It says 'Brut' but is only just dry; pale, soft and fizzily orchardy, with 11% alcohol.

SPAIN

8 **Taste the Difference Vintage Cava 2008** £8.99
The majority Chardonnay in this blend makes itself felt with creamy apple flavours in a nice plush fizz.

8 **Marques de Montoya Vintage Cava Rosé**
2009 £10.99
Party-frock pink, brut-style, crisply fresh, strawberry-tangy sparkler of merit. Don't let the naff label deter you.

Tesco

Half the wines among the 70 I have picked out at Tesco this year are from the 'Finest' range of own-labels. It figures. They bear the Tesco name and carry the reputation of the retail giant with them, so the people responsible take them seriously. You might expect the wines to be safe and generic – claret, Australian Chardonnay and so on – but in fact many of them are commendably off the wall. Among my particular favourites this year is Finest Teroldego, a red wine from a thoroughly esoteric grape made in the foothills of Italy's Dolomites. More familiar, but just as much of a surprise, is Finest Soave. This dry Veronese white can these days feel like a throwback to the 1950s, but the one that the Tesco team has found is a real Soave, a modern classic, and at a realistic price.

Italy has been one of Tesco's strong suits for as long as I can remember. But the range – both of branded wines and of own-labels – from Australia seems suddenly to have taken off too. France is well represented, and I must mention the dinky 'single serve' Languedoc wines lately introduced under the Finest brand in 18.7cl bottles. They might resemble airline offerings, but the wines are of terrific quality.

Be warned that by no means all the wines I have recommended here will be available in all Tesco stores. There is great variation, according to the size and location of your local outlet. But a big proportion of the overall range is available through the Tesco wine website. It's case sales only – six-bottle cases mainly – and delivery (of a minimum of one six-bottle case) is amazingly efficient. Order before noon and they guarantee next-day delivery during the week.

The website is a handy source of information on the perpetual discounts Tesco offers on its wines. You get the same savings online as you would get in store, plus numerous online special offers on wines stocked in only a few outlets, if any. Do have a look at the 'Fine Wine' list which is exclusively online and now runs to about 300 items, including classed growth clarets at up to £1,500 for a six-bottle case.

Unlike most of the competition, Tesco regularly discounts its own-label wines, including the Finest range. I believe these wines are fairly priced in the first place (I wouldn't otherwise give them space), so when they are cut – even halved – in price they are genuine bargains. In this respect, among others, Tesco is a very sensible place in which to shop for wine.

Red Wines

ARGENTINA

🍷 10 Broquel Bonarda 2009   £10.99
Bumper beetrooty lavish smoothie by big Mendoza winery Trapiche has a naff label, but from the blood-red colour to the ideal marriage of fruit-and-vanilla richness with beautifully judged dry abrasion, it is an outstanding special-occasion wine that does owe some of its style to the Italian origins of its grape, the rare Bonarda; 14.5% alcohol.

🍷 6 Beachcomber Low Alcohol Red   £5.00
Curious customers with temperance tendencies might like to know that this 5.5% alcohol Shiraz/Cabernet mix tastes like wine mixed with grape juice.

AUSTRALIA

🍷 10 Finest Block 19 Shiraz Cabernet Sauvignon
2009   £7.99
Boot-black monster Barossa with 93% Shiraz and 14.5% alcohol is robust with tight liquorice intensity and sweet, roasted black fruit. It's lush, savoury and soothing, with extraordinary poise at this sort of price.

🍷 8 Finest Block 13 Shiraz Grenache 2008   £8.99
Rich, smoky comforter from cult McLaren Vale winery d'Arenberg makes a savoury winter warmer with a nice orange-pith twang at the finish.

🍷 9 Morse Code Shiraz 2009   £8.99
Generous, complete ripe wine has lifted fruit and ideal weight, and combines juiciness with spice and savouriness en route to a trim, gripping finish; 14% alcohol.

Red Wines

FRANCE

🍷 8 Château La R
Deep purple, enga
from more than on
appeal.

🍷 8 Malbec Les
From leading Ca
nicely packaged,
muscular black-f

🍷 10 Finest Bo
2009
Pale but who
presages an
elegantly ripe
with a good g
already mello
the best of all

🍷 9 Châte
Lush, leafy
Anjou taste
lot of ju
andard.

Fin
bu
ea

RED WINES

9 Bellariva

Limpid Beaujo[...]
winery De Bor[...]
juiciness and g[...]

AUSTRALIA

8 Madba[...]

Putting a zan[...]
at your own [...]
McDonald, [...]
spicy black-f[...]

9 Tim [...]

Artful mell[...]
with spicy [...]
it is opuler[...]

CHILE

8 End[...]
20[...]

Wholeso[...]
raspberr[...]

FRANCE

8 F[...]
1[...]

Tiny b[...]
colour [...]
Unexp[...]

9

Healt[...]
fruit, [...]
heral[...]

RED WINES

FRANCE

9 Chapoutier Gigondas 2007 £16.79

This tarry, silky, creamy Rhône classic with chocolate centre from a rightly rated maturing vintage is an absolute treat; 14.5% alcohol.

10 Châteauneuf du Pape Gonnet Frères 2007 £19.99

Immaculate ripe and spicy wine from famed Châteauneuf property Font de Michelle is already well developed and brimming with dark, complex, discreetly oaked savoury fruit; 14.5% alcohol. This is serious wine from a superb vintage, and not overpriced.

ITALY

10 Finest Teroldego Vigneti Delle Dolomiti 2009 £5.99

Terrific violet-scented sub-Alpine red from the obscure Teroldego grape has vivacious, crisp, leafy redcurrant freshness; it is made by Italian mega-producer Cavit but seems to me none the worse for it. Very keenly priced into the bargain.

7 Finest Valpolicella Ripasso 2009 £6.99

Coffee note in this quirky black-cherry speciality wine, which could do with time to round out.

9 Finest Barbera d'Asti 2007 £7.49

Silky, dark, blueberry-fruit bouncer from Piedmont[...]
misty hills is a perennial favourite, with gravitas as w[...]
as perfect pasta-matching juiciness.

RED WINES

9 **Piccini Memoro** £8.99

A blend of four grape varieties from four Italian regions and several vintages, made in Tuscany by suitably ubiquitous producer Piccini, this is a dark, savoury, seductive 14%-alcohol oaked red with a saucy butterscotch trace and a lot of Italian charm.

9 **Monte Nobile Squinzano Riserva 2007** £9.99

Ripe, cherry-chocolate Puglian smoothie in a spiffingly heraldic bottle with screwtop is a frequent bargain on discount.

9 **Gran Conti Rosso del Molise 2006** £10.99

Juicy and plump, this Adriatic mix of Montepulciano and Aglianico has beguiling ripe strawberry fruit with savoury, truffly, spicy richness and a dry, nutty finish. Variously labelled as either DOC Molise or DOC Rosso di Biferno, but of very consistent charm and regularly on offer at half price.

8 **Terre di Priori Brunello di Montalcino 2006** £19.99

A sort of super Chianti, this is going gently brown and delivers the sort of lush, mocha, pure-silk minty sleekness you are entitled to expect for the money.

8 **Finest Touriga Nacional 2010** £7.79

I like this cheery, raspberry-bright Alentejo raspberry rasper; lively, eager and fresh, it does well from the fridge with rich fish dishes and sticky pasta.

8 **First Cape Discovery Series Merlot 2010** £6.99

Juicy black-cherry fruit fills out this dry and brisk, well-made party red; very likeable.

ITALY

PORTUGAL

ROMANIA

RED WINES

SOUTH AFRICA

8 **Finest Stellenbosch Shiraz 2009** £7.99
Typically tarry and minty Cape meat-matcher has pleasing spicy abrasion and 14% alcohol.

8 **Greenfields Organic Shiraz
Cabernet Sauvignon 2010** £8.49
Healthy-tasting Stellenbosch blend with straight blackcurrant fruit and a gentle tannin grip; 14% alcohol, but not at all over-ripe, as some Cape Cabernet can be.

SPAIN

8 **Baron de Ley Graciano 2009** £8.99
Rioja from Graciano, a grape variety long out of favour in the region but now making some interesting, intense, deeply coloured, blackcurranty oaked reds – this is a good introduction.

8 **Finest Viña Mara Rioja Reserva 2006** £9.49
Crème brûleé nose on this dark, maturing pure Tempranillo matches the creamy-pruny flavour; might just dry out quite soon.

USA

8 **Finest Alexander Cabernet Sauvignon 2009** £8.99
Distinctly New World style to this generous and sunny Californian with appealing blackcurrant ripeness and tannic structure; 14.5% alcohol.

PINK WINES

AUSTRALIA

6 **Beachcomber Low Alcohol Rosé** £5.00
Plausible prickly pink with plenty of sugar and 5.5%
alcohol just about qualifies as wine.

PORTUGAL

7 **Finest Touriga Nacional Rosé 2010** £6.99
Dense pink colour and cassis fruit in this Lisbon
confection from the principal grape in port production.

SPAIN

8 **Finest Navarra Rosé 2010** £6.99
Cherry-magenta Garnacha tastes pleasingly pink and
healthy, and briskly dry until you get a parting lick of
residual sugar.

WHITE WINES

ARGENTINA

7 **Finest Torrontes 2010** £8.99
Muscatty but dry exotic wine from Argentina's signature
indigenous grape with 15% Sauvignon added for zing;
distinctive, but a shade pricy, I think.

AUSTRALIA

6 **Banrock Station Light Chardonnay
Sauvignon Blanc 2011** £5.49
Alcohol-lite (5.5%) confection tastes more like wine than
some, with a curious ersatz sweetness.

8 **Sketches Chardonnay Semillon 2010** £7.99
Ripe pineappley aromas give way to an exotic fruit blend
with sweet-apple Chardonnay at centre in this unoaked,
thoughtful aperitif dry white.

WHITE WINES

Tesco

AUSTRALIA

**⏛ 8 Finest Boranup Sauvignon Blanc Semillon
2010**   £9.99
Nettly freshness to this juicily gooseberryish Western
Australian quencher with a sly tropical note.

⏛ 8 Finest Denman Semillon 2010   £9.99
Crafty balance of tropical fruit and citrus twang in this
Hunter Valley charmer with just 10.5% alcohol.

⏛ 8 Tahbilk Cellar Selection Marsanne 2008   £9.99
Toast-and-butter dry white from famed Victoria
estate teams grassy freshness with leesy (but unoaked)
creaminess. Shellfish wine.

⏛ 9 Tim Adams Clare Valley Semillon 2009   £11.29
'Parsnips and lime,' I wrote mysteriously in the note on
this complex, new-oaked dry and sublimely mineral wine.
You get pineapple and peach, and preternatural freshness
too.

AUSTRIA

⏛ 8 Finest Grüner Veltliner 2010   £6.99
Aromatic and esoteric green-valley wine is notably dry
and crisp; stands out from the crowd.

CHILE

⏛ 9 Emiliana 'O' Viognier 2010   £7.99
Spot-on rich-but-zesty aperitif is extravagant in colour
and sweet-blossom perfume, and balanced with sunny
ripeness and citrus finish.

**⏛ 8 Casa Silva Angostura Gran Reserva
Chardonnay 2010**   £12.99
Luxury oaked tropical-fruit Chardonnay of the old school
has proverbial harmony between ripeness and refreshment,
with 14% alcohol. Would be nice with lobster.

WHITE WINES

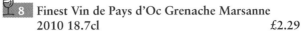

8 **Finest Vin de Pays d'Oc Grenache Marsanne**
   2010 18.7cl £2.29
Single-serve bottle reveals a super dry white with a positive
veggie-basket of fresh, rooty, white-fruit flavours; if only
airline wine was this good.

9 **Tesco Mâcon-Villages 2010** £4.89
Yet another excellent house Mâcon with good colour,
spearmint/lemon-drop nose and crunchy-apple
Chardonnay fruit with freshness and zest, all at a very
keen price.

9 **Finest Picpoul de Pinet 2010** £7.29
Attractively packaged Mediterranean seafood-matcher
is hefty by prevailing standards, with exemplary lemon
tanginess and seaside freshness.

8 **Finest White Burgundy 2010** £7.79
Agreeable hint of buttery scrambled egg on this unoaked,
mineral Chardonnay charmer.

8 **Tesco Chablis 2009** £7.79
Proper chalky-mineral Chablis whiff and tangy, typical
flinty Chardonnay style.

9 **Château La Rezé Organic Minervois Blanc**
   2010 £8.99
Don't let the hopelessly old-fashioned labelling of this
lush Mediterranean wine put you off. It's gold in colour
with deliciously developed ripe white-fruit flavours,
creamily oaked.

WHITE WINES

8 **Finest Bourgogne Hautes Côtes de Beaune 2009** £9.29
Vanilla oak enhances the lifted fresh sweet-apple fruit in this artfully lemon-edged burgundy.

9 **Finest Chablis 2009** £9.99
Love this flinty and reassuringly recognisable Chablis with its balance between crisp Chardonnay definition and creamy ripeness.

9 **Blason de Bourgogne St Véran 2009** £10.49
Deservedly popular brand's big, lush Mâconnais is a great treat, unoaked but lavishly ripe and rewarding.

8 **Finest Meursault 2008** £20.79
If you're going buy supermarket Meursault, make it this one, a traditional barrel-fermented, richly coloured and mellow Chardonnay with fine balance.

9 **Finest Soave Classico Superiore 2009** £6.99
I kept coming back to this; beguiling, well-coloured Verona dry white has big fruit flavours with peachiness and blanched-almond richness, neatly balanced with a citrus edginess. Serious stuff.

8 **Finest Vermentino 2010** £6.99
Generous dry Sicilian has tangy freshness and a supporting nutty intensity.

8 **Finest Gavi 2010** £8.29
Noticeably lemony example of this chic Piedmont dry white with ripe-apple freshness and a little creamy richness.

WHITE WINES

ITALY

8 **Finest Falanghina 2010** £8.99

Lots of autumn orchard fruit in this Puglian brisk dry food wine with a good heft and what seems a slightly elevated price.

9 **Lava Greco di Tufo 2010** £12.99

From Italy's enchanted Campania, an extraordinary dry, mineral aperitif white with a wholesome hint of brimstone from the volcanic soil of a region in thrall to Vesuvius, which is quaintly depicted on the label.

NEW ZEALAND

8 **Finest Marlborough Sauvignon Blanc 2011** £9.99

Nettles and gooseberries are to the fore in this fun package of briny freshness from the new vintage.

9 **Thornbury Riesling 2008** £10.99

Straw-gold colour, limey scent and plenty of plump fruit in this Moselle-evoking Kiwi contrivance with a racy minerality all its own.

SOUTH AFRICA

8 **Zalze Chenin Blanc 2011** £6.99

Fresh, near-fizzing dry, but sneakily honeyed style to this Stellenbosch aperitif wine.

10 **Finest Ken Forrester Chenin Blanc 2010** £7.99

I am a complete sucker for this generous, part-barrel-fermented Cape perennial; ritzy colour and aromas of fruit blossom with nectar notes flow into an eagerly fresh rush of orchardy flavours finishing dry and very moreish. Brilliant.

8 **Sauvignon.com 2011** £7.99

Bizarrely named Western Cape creation for the digital age has lots of lush-grass appeal.

WHITE WINES

SPAIN

🍷 7 **Finest Albariño 2010** £7.79
Big-flavoured varietal from Rias Baixas on the Atlantic west coast has seaside freshness with a lick of foreign sweetness.

SPARKLING WINES

FRANCE

🍷 8 **Finest Blanquette de Limoux 1531 2008** £9.99
Attractive tiny-bubble mousse in this vintage Pyrenean fizz carries brisk, sunny flavours; 1531 is allegedly the date the first sparkling Limoux was made, long before champagne.

🍷 9 **Finest Premier Cru Champagne** £19.99
Soft, beguiling, bready brut champagne from top-rated *premier cru* vineyards has instant appeal and the mellowness of bottle-ageing. A crowd-pleaser at a fair price.

🍷 8 **Finest Vintage Champagne 2004** £25.99
You get a convincing contrapuntal thrill from the eager freshness versus the mellow richness in this craftily contrived all-Chardonnay champagne; the premium price is warranted.

ITALY

🍷 8 **Finest Bisol Prosecco di Valdobbiadene** £9.99
Smart-looking and authentic dry vigorous Veneto sparkler has lively orchard fruit.

Waitrose

 The first wine of more than 200 lined up for the monster Waitrose tasting this year was Bolney Estate Foxhole Vineyard Pinot Noir 2010. I liked it, and had written a note before looking to see where it came from. 'Maybe the Mâconnais,' I thought.

But the Bolney Estate, it turns out, is about half an hour from Brighton, in Sussex. Yes, this is English wine, and English red wine at that. The only clue had been the price – £11.99. English wines are rarely cheap. And in my experience, I fear, the still wines are seldom interesting either. But this one is. Typical of Waitrose to find an off-beat item like this.

The Waitrose range is simply enormous, with more than 1,000 wines lined up in the book-sized, colour-illustrated catalogues periodically issued each year. And uniquely among the major supermarkets, you can count on most of the wines being available from most of the stores, most of the time. I suppose it helps that Waitrose has a relatively modest number of branches – a mere 230 around the UK.

For those few who are still without a handy branch, Waitrose Wine Direct is a crisply usable and comprehensive website from which you can order any mix of the wines for home delivery. Minimum order is 12 bottles and you get a 5 per cent discount, as you would if you bought any 6 bottles in store. Next-day delivery costs £6.95.

Waitrose's upmarket profile does not prevent it discounting wines with the same persistence and enthusiasm employed by its brasher competitors. And what's more, a lot of the discounts are quite obviously the real thing. So do have a

squint at the wines on promo when you pop in. Waitrose wine prices are entirely competitive on an everyday basis – and I struggle to believe this isn't true of most of the grocery items in these stores – and the discounted wines are often among the best bargains in any of the supermarkets.

Is Waitrose still the best supermarket for wine? To my way of thinking, definitely yes.

RED WINES

ARGENTINA

 8 **Norton Reserva Malbec 2008**   £10.99
Benchmark Mendoza Malbec is deep, deep purple with
roasted (not scorched) plummy-spicy ripeness and 14.5%
alcohol. Would like beef.

8 **Penfolds Koonunga Hill Shiraz/
         Cabernet Sauvignon 2008**   £8.99
A revisit to one of South Australia's earliest export brands
finds a familiar electric soup of dark, plummy delights in
convincing balance.

AUSTRALIA

8 **See Saw Shiraz/Mourvèdre 2009**   £8.99
It's 95% Shiraz from the Hunter and Barossa Valleys and
a cheery, fruit-and-nut, spiced, chocolate-hearted, nicely
weighted varietal of real character.

9 **Jim Barry Clare Red Shiraz/
         Cabernet Sauvignon 2006**   £10.99
Lovely assured 70/30% blend is ideally balanced between
vivid black fruit and appetising abrasion. It's still grippy
as well as mellow in maturity, and wears its 14.5%
alcohol lightly.

8 **Stonier Pinot Noir 2009**   £12.99
The name Stonier (on Victoria's Mornington Peninsula)
hints at the the mineral quality of this pure-tasting, slick,
summer-fruit Pinot. A very likeable, natural wine.

BULGARIA

8 **Enira 2007**   £9.99
Mostly Merlot from Thrace, the colour is ruby going
peaty and the fruit is mellow and plush with a dark-
chocolate core; at 15% alcohol, a big Bulgarian beastie.

RED WINES

8 **Doña Dominga Single Vineyard Shiraz 2010 £7.49**
Spicy but refined dark and firm Colchagua wine is long, blackberry pure and trim at the finish.

8 **Valdivieso Winemaker Reserva Malbec 2010** £7.49
This inky purple, big-nosed (raspberry syrup), wild briar-fruit, clingy-friendly food red finishes tight and dry.

9 **Torres Las Mulas Cabernet Sauvignon 2009** £8.99
Catalan genius Miguel Torres excels in Chile, so this new organic wine is predictably good: lush, leafy, creamy (new oak) and wholesome pure-fruit flavours with controlled ripeness.

CHILE

8 **Bolney Estate Foxhole Vineyard Pinot Noir 2010** £11.99
Sussex burgundy? It has a pale oniony colour and convincing raspberry notes, along with pepper and lemon in the background, and is quite substantial in weight. My only problem is the price.

ENGLAND

9 **Cuvée Chasseur 2010** £4.35
Perennial Béziers bargain from Carignan and Grenache is attractively bouncy with squishy hedgerow fruit and perky freshness. Cannot fault it, especially for value.

8 **Good Ordinary Claret 2010** £4.49
Meaningful mauve colour, chocolate-blueberry fondant nose and nice ripe brambly gripping fruit. And cheap!

FRANCE

RED WINES

8 **Chat-en-Oeuf 2010** £5.49

Popular Languedoc brand from Grenache and Syrah is darkly minty, spicy and grippy and 14% alcohol. Real wine, not just a gimmicky package.

8 **Laforêt Beaujolais 2010** £7.49

Peardrop whiff does not detract from the squished-raspberry charm of this fresh, drink-cool, juicy wine; a good harbinger for the 2010 vintage.

8 **Bouchard Aîné et Fils Red Burgundy 2009** £8.99

Sleek raspberry fruit in this sunnily ripe Gamay–Pinot Noir mix has a toasty centre from lavish new-oak ageing. Try with fish pie.

9 **Guigal Côtes du Rhône 2007** £9.99

I'm amazed that the great '07 vintage of this classic CdR has not already sold out. Buy now: it's slinky, gamey, mature, spicy and luxuriously oaked. Very seductive.

9 **Laurent Miquel L'Atelier Grenache/Syrah/Mourvèdre 2008** £9.99

Angular Pays d'Oc gripper with sweet-oaked plump fruit is savoury and friendly.

9 **Chinon Les Complices de Loire Les Graviers 2009** £10.99

Deep purple colour and strong grippy-twiggy brambly fruit in this smooth and hefty Chinon; built to last but deliciously fresh and appealing right now.

FRANCE

RED WINES

FRANCE

🍷 **8** **Esprit de Puisseguin 2009** £10.99
Rich, ripe claret from the satellite St Emilion AC of Puisseguin has dark berry fruit, silky smoothness and a long future. Good already, though.

🍷 **8** **Château L'Hospitalet La Réserve 2009** £11.99
Dense, blood-red La Clape, Languedoc red is both lively and lavish; darkly spicy and 14.5% alcohol.

🍷 **9** **Château Maris Les Vieilles Vignes 2009** £12.99
Lovely big silky liquorice fruit bomb from esoteric AC of Minervois La Livinière is pitch dark and wildly savoury with garrigue herb and spice and 15% alcohol. Sounds a bit of a handful, but is very easy indeed to relish.

🍷 **9** **Givry Domaine Besson Le Haut Colombier 2009** £14.99
Extravagant mineral southern burgundy has a big sweet strawberry nose and generous, supple classic Pinot Noir earthy-minty appeal.

ITALY

🍷 **8** **Moncaro Rosso Piceno Superiore 2010** £4.99
Dense and sweetly ripe but balanced blend of Montepulciano and Sangiovese from the Marches is charming, and finishes neatly clean.

🍷 **8** **Vignale Valpolicella 2010** £4.99
You get a proper cherry blast on the nose of this vivacious Verona refresher, then a generous helping of strawberry in the fruit. Super pizza red, and good served cool.

RED WINES

9 Saluti Vino Rosso £5.99
A blend of Sicilian and mainland fruit from a blend of
vintages, this is charmingly juicy, toasty and rounded with
textbook balance and dry finish. I really warmed to it.

8 Siciliano Wild Cat Nero d'Avola 2009 £6.49
Chocolate depths to the black fruit in this lively and
artfully abrasive island wine to sip with pungent salami
and pongy cheese.

10 Inycon Nero d'Avola/Frappato 2010 £6.69
Sicilian wine hits the spot by tasting wildly fruity in that
sun-baked island way of Sicily, but also opulent, toasty
and rich. It tastes way above price. Grapy juiciness and
black-fruit gravitas in perfect harmony. I love it.

8 Chianti Poggiotondo Cerro del Masso 2008 £8.99
Firmly defined Chianti has dark, near-baked fruit just
short of raisiny; a grown-up, riserva style.

8 Paolo Leo Primitivo di Manduria 2009 £9.99
An expensive-looking bottle for this Salento (Puglia)
heavyweight with 14.5% alcohol; blood-red, dense,
baked black fruit with bitter-chocolate centre – a serious
winter warmer.

8 Barbaresco Cantina del Pino 2007 £26.99
Madly expensive but entirely authentic Piedmont classic
is irresistibly redolent of coffee and petits fours; pellucid,
mature and balanced, even with 14.5% alcohol.

RED WINES

ITALY

8 **Alois Lageder Krafuss Pinot Noir 2007** £27.99
From Alpine Italy, a mature wine with a streak of orange in its pale colour and a perplexing wet-dishcloth note in the sweet-cherry nose, but a fascinating, elegant, self-assured Pinot of great poise to compare with good burgundy.

NEW ZEALAND

7 **Brancott Estate Pinot Noir 2009** £10.99
Brancott is the daft new name of Kiwi giant Montana, and this is a nice, pale, edgy, earthy pure-fruit Pinot – but expensive.

9 **Craggy Range Merlot 2008** £14.99
From the lately revered Gimblett Gravels of Hawke's Bay, a gorgeous, silky, new-oak de luxe eucalyptus ripe (14% alcohol) and ready wine; a kind of Kiwi Pomerol.

PORTUGAL

8 **Vida Nova Tinto 2008** £8.99
Cliff Richard's Algarve Syrah is very dark and ripe, even roasty, with well-defined spicy black fruit.

8 **Cortes de Cima Syrah 2008** £11.49
Very ripe (14% alcohol) Alentejo, slinky, dark, minty-sappy wine made me think of the Madeira 'burn' flavour from the estufagem heating process; a curiously likeable, thoroughly Portuguese red.

ROMANIA

9 **La Umbra Merlot 2009** £5.99
Mouthfuls of morello cherries with a leafy edge to the ripeness in this Carpathian bargain; extravagant but balanced, with 14% alcohol. Romania is back.

RED WINES

SOUTH AFRICA

🍷 8 **Vredenhof Cellar Reserve**
Cabernet Sauvignon 2010   £6.79
Toasty-tarry typical Cape liquorice Cabernet with 14%
alcohol and a sensible price.

🍷 8 **Zalze Shiraz-Mourvèdre-Viognier 2010**   £6.99
Spicy-savoury oaked blend with agreeable weight and
14.5% alcohol works well.

🍷 9 **Cederberg Waitrose Foundation Shiraz**
2009   £7.99
Poised, spicy gripper with dark, plummy ripeness (14.5%
alcohol) has a pleasing weight and definition. A share of
the profits goes back into the community at Cederberg, a
mountain region 200 miles north of Cape Town.

🍷 9 **Rustenberg John X Merriman 2008**   £12.49
Ooh, what a lovely lush and toasty claret-style smoothie
from the Stellenbosch; it's elegant and restrained, even
with 14.5% alcohol. It's easy to overlook SA's knack for
making top-flight reds.

SPAIN

🍷 8 **Navarra Viña del Perdon Gran Reserva**
2000   £9.99
Gently browning old Merlot/Cabernet has oxidative
charms, the dark fruit still juicy over the vanilla of three
years in oak.

PINK WINES

9 **Torres Las Mulas Cabernet Sauvignon Rosé 2010** £8.99
Glowing magenta colour and strawberries on the nose make this a very enticing prospect; corresponding ripe, sweet fruit balanced by tangy acidity fulfil expectations.

8 **Viña Leyda Loica Vineyard Pinot Noir Rosé 2010** £9.99
Smoked-salmon colour, soft summer-fruit nose and crisp raspberry fruit.

8 **Abbotts Reserve Grenache Rosé 2010** £6.99
Bold, dry strawberry Languedoc pink has a fleeting saucy sweetness that does not diminish its appeal.

7 **Champteloup Rosé d'Anjou 2010** £6.99
Easy, ripe, sweet-but-brisk strawberry Loire pink has just 11% alcohol.

8 **Mirabeau Provence Rosé 2010** £8.99
Sunny coral colour with rosy, crunchily dry, fresh fruit revealing apples and blackberry alike; intriguing.

8 **Fattoria Nicodemi Cerasuolo Montepulciano d'Abruzzo 2010** £9.29
Magenta wine's fruit is blackcurrant-dominated, strong and dry-finishing; assertive food pink.

8 **Southbank Estate Sauvignon Blanc Rosé 2010** £8.99
Made by adding a bucket of Syrah to a tank of Sauvignon, this is a tangy gooseberry, pale salmon pink of likeable zestiness.

CHILE

FRANCE

ITALY

N. ZEALAND

PINK WINES

8 **Gran López Tempranillo Rosado 2010** £4.99
Shocking pink colour and brambly-orchardy fruit are fun
and good value in this craftily made lick-of-sweetness but
ostensibly dry La Mancha cheapie.

WHITE WINES

8 **De Bortoli DB Selection Verdelho 2010** £6.49
Dry, grassy, but lush partly oaked refresher in the style of
the great dry whites of Spain's Galicia, and a very decent
tilt at it. Dull label does this no favours.

8 **Petaluma Riesling 2008** £10.99
Exotic oxidative Clare Valley limey Riesling is already
petrolly, and deliciously so.

8 **Waitrose Chilean Sauvignon Blanc 2010** £7.69
Keen, green, but not lean, nettly dry refresher by
Valdivieso.

7 **Chapel Down Flint Dry 2010** £8.99
Flintier and drier than in earlier years, this Kent wine in
the Loire style is progressing; 11.5% alcohol.

8 **Cuvée Pêcheur 2010** £4.35
Perennial Gers bargain is fresh and orchardy, lemony but
not tart, and keenly refreshing.

9 **Cave de Lugny Chardonnay 2010** £6.99
Nice cabbagey Mâconnais is new-grass fresh with a
peachy ripeness. I retasted it twice and liked it better and
better as a bargain white burgundy.

WHITE WINES

8 Fief Guérin Muscadet Côtes de Grandlieu
Sur Lie 2010 £6.99
Briny-lemony Loire moules-matcher is an acquired taste,
but good of its kind.

8 Champteloup Sauvignon Blanc 2010 £7.79
Squeaky-green and briny Touraine zinger is impressively
full-fruited and ripe.

9 Picpoul de Pinet Domaine Félines 2010 £7.99
The biggest Picpoul of the year, this is gold in colour
with full but tangy white fruits of real ripeness; untypical
maybe, but dimensionally delicious.

8 Domaine de la Fruitière Cuvée Muscadet
Sèvre et Maine 2005 £9.99
Muscadet is supposed to be glugged in its first flush of
youth. This one is positively geriatric, but great fun: gold
colour, lush with white orchardy fruit hinting at toffee
apple, and clean edged; how about lobster?

7 Waitrose Chablis 2010 £10.49
Plenty of proverbial gunflint in this spanking new co-
op-made Chablis with the principal merit of tasting like
Chablis; mineral, just short of austere, it might develop.

9 Paul Zinck Riesling Eichberg Grand Cru
2007 £14.99
Esoteric Alsace is limey-dry but exotically aromatic,
generously coloured, piled high with mineral-racy flavour
and a classic of its rare kind.

WHITE WINES

FRANCE

8 **Pernand-Vergelesses Domaine Jean-Jacques Girard Les Belles Filles 2009** **£16.99**
A big, yellow burgundy poised between plush and fresh, with plenty of exotic, mineral Chardonnay character to fill the space. Loved it.

8 **Chassagne-Montrachet Premier Cru Louis Jadot 2008** **£26.99**
Names to be reckoned with, and a safe buy for that extra-special occasion; this is quite strict and correct pure mineral oak-fermented Chardonnay.

GERMANY

9 **Dr Wagner Riesling 2010** **£8.99**
Water-white but powerfully perfumed apple-blossom Moselle is whizzingly fresh with a dollop of honey in the centre of the flavour; 8.5% alcohol.

9 **Dr Loosen Urziger Würzgarten Riesling Kabinett 2010** **£13.99**
Masses of apple fruit and mineral raciness in this super river-fresh Moselle with just 7.6% alcohol.

HUNGARY

8 **Mátra Mountain Pinot Grigio 2010** **£5.99**
Flinty-fresh and smoky dry wine from what is reported to be Europe's largest PG vineyard (what a prospect!); a match for Veneto PGs any time.

ITALY

8 **Trinacria Bianco 2010** **£3.99**
Well-coloured, plump and earthy-dry throwing wine from Sicily finishes clean and will suit creamy pastas as well as stand-up occasions.

WHITE WINES

7 Soave Vignale 2010 £4.89

Grassy not green, sweet not sugary, almondy not soggy, recognisably Soave – which is a plus at this price.

8 Birgi Grillo 2010 £4.99

Cicada on the label does put you in mind of Sicily, where this nice, flinty dry white hails from; long, likeable vegetal flavours refresh.

8 La Monetta Gavi di Gavi 2010 £9.99

Richly coloured, mineral-nutty, balanced, trendy Piedmont dry white has distinctive vegetal qualities and lush freshness.

8 Cowrie Bay Chardonnay 2010 £5.99

Untypically cheap, Kiwi sweet-apple lightly oaked Chardonnay from Montana (now called Brancott) giant is mild-mannered but fresh and alluring.

9 Tiki Ridge Sauvignon Blanc Reserve 2010 £8.99

High colour and strong asparagus pong to this generously ripe Marlborough lush-grass number; stands out.

10 Fairview La Capra Chardonnay 2010 £7.99

Buttery scrambled egg richness in this lush Cox's apple wine with 14% alcohol; the balance is brilliant, and it tastes way above its price. By Fairtrade pioneer Charles Back.

9 Rustenberg Chardonnay 2010 £12.49

Rich and mineral harmonious Chardonnay from Stellenbosch has 14.5% alcohol, but well-judged weight and a fine, clean, limey edge.

WHITE WINES

SPAIN

8 **Gran López Airén/Sauvignon Blanc 2010** **£4.99**
Do I smell primroses? Easy, light, 11.5% alcohol La Mancha refresher with sunny appeal.

8 **Viña Taboexa Albariño Rias Baixas 2010** **£9.99**
Understated but convincing rush-of-seagrass, fresh, dry wine from Galicia.

USA

8 **Delicato Fog Head Chardonnay 2009** **£14.99**
Curiously named Monterey, California, wine is luscious with lifted apple-pie (and cream) fruit; makes a lasting impression with its elegant balance.

SPARKLING WINES

ENGLAND

8 **Ridgeview Merret Bloomsbury 2008** **£21.99**
Plenty of colour and yeasty aroma in this Chardonnay–Pinot (champagne-style) blend from Sussex with enough bottle age to mellow it. It ain't champagne, but it's quite convincing.

8 **Nyetimber Classic Cuvée 2006** **£29.99**
I could easily fall for this one as a champagne; it's from Sussex Chardonnay and Pinots and has a fine mousse, decent colour and bready, mellow character; even the price conforms to its French counterpart.

FRANCE

8 **Ackerman Sparkling Cabernet Franc Brut Rosé** **£7.99**
Candy-floss pink Loire fizz has oodles of strawberry flavour but comes out dry and niftily fresh.

SPARKLING WINES

FRANCE

9 Waitrose Blanc de Noirs Champagne Brut £18.99
Generously coloured brioche-nosed mellow, rounded, all-Pinot Noir champagne of very evident class; like it much more than Waitrose's standard Brut.

ITALY

7 San Leo Prosecco Brut £8.99
Soft, grapy fruit and soft mousse, but it does finish dry.

N. ZEALAND

9 Lindauer Sauvignon Blanc Brut £9.99
Maybe it's the novelty that impressed me so much, but I loved this exuberant nettly-gooseberry Sauvignon with bubbles; it tastes exactly as you'd expect.

What wine
words mean

Wine labels are getting crowded. It's mostly thanks to the unending torrent of new regulation. Lately, for example, the European Union has decided that all wines sold within its borders must display a health warning: 'Contains Sulphites'. All wines are made with the aid of preparations containing sulphur to combat diseases in the vineyards and bacterial infections in the winery. You can't make wine without sulphur. Even 'organic' wines are made with it. But some people are sensitive to the traces of sulphur in some wines, so we must all be informed of the presence of this hazardous material.

That's the way it is. And it might not be long before some even sterner warnings will be added about another ingredient in wine. Alcohol is the new tobacco, as the regulators see it, and in the near future we can look forward to some stern admonishments about the effects of alcohol. In the meantime, the mandatory information on every label includes the quantity, alcoholic strength and country of origin, along with the name of the producer. The region will be specified, vaguely on wines from loosely regulated countries such as Australia, and precisely on wines from over-regulated countries such as France. Wines from 'classic' regions of Europe – Bordeaux, Chianti, Rioja and so on – are mostly labelled according to their location rather than their constituent grape varieties. If it says Sancerre, it's taken as read that you either know it's made with Sauvignon Blanc grapes, or don't care.

Wines from just about everywhere else make no such assumptions. If a New Zealand wine is made from Sauvignon Blanc grapes, you can be sure the label will say so. This does quite neatly represent the gulf between the two worlds of winemaking. In traditional European regions, it's the place, the vineyard, that mostly determines the character of the wines. The French call it terroir, to encapsulate not just the lie of the land and the soil conditions but the wild variations in the weather from year to year as well. The grapes are merely the medium through which the timeless mysteries of the deep earth are translated into the ineffable glories of the wine, adjusted annually according to the vagaries of climate, variable moods of the winemaker, and who knows what else.

In the less arcane vineyards of the New World, the grape is definitely king. In hot valleys such as the Barossa (South Australia) or the Maipo (Chile), climate is relatively predictable and the soil conditions are managed by irrigation. It's the fruit that counts, and the style of the wine is determined by the variety – soft, spicy Shiraz; peachy, yellow Chardonnay and so on.

The main purpose of this glossary is, consequently, to give short descriptions of the 'classic' wines, including the names of the grapes they are made from, and of the 70-odd distinct grape varieties that make most of the world's wines. As well as these very brief descriptions, I have included equally shortened summaries of the regions and appellations of the better-known wines, along with some of the local terms used to indicate style and alleged qualities.

Finally, I have tried to explain in simple and rational terms the peculiar words I use in trying to convey the characteristics of wines described. 'Delicious' might need no further qualification, but the likes of 'bouncy', 'green' and 'liquorous' probably do.

A

abboccato – Medium-dry white wine style. Italy, especially Orvieto.

AC – *See* Appellation d'Origine Contrôlée.

acidity – To be any good, every wine must have the right level of acidity. It gives wine the element of dryness or sharpness it needs to prevent cloying sweetness or dull wateriness. If there is too much acidity, wine tastes raw or acetic (vinegary). Winemakers strive to create balanced acidity – either by cleverly controlling the natural processes, or by adding sugar and acid to correct imbalances.

aftertaste – The flavour that lingers in the mouth after swallowing the wine.

Aglianico – Black grape variety of southern Italy. It has romantic associations. When the ancient Greeks first colonised Italy in the seventh century BC, it was with the prime purpose of planting it as a vineyard (the Greek name for Italy was *Oenotria* – land of cultivated vines). The name for the vines the Greeks brought with them was Ellenico (as in Hellas, Greece), from which Aglianico is the modern rendering. To return to the point, these ancient vines, especially in the arid volcanic landscapes of Basilicata and Cilento, produce excellent dark, earthy and highly distinctive wines. A name to look out for.

Agriculture biologique – On French wine labels, an indication that the wine has been made by organic methods.

Albariño – White grape variety of Spain that makes intriguingly perfumed fresh and spicy dry wines, especially in esteemed Rias Baixas region.

alcohol – The alcohol levels in wines are expressed in terms of alcohol by volume ('abv'), that is, the percentage of the volume of the wine that is common, or ethyl, alcohol. A typical wine at 12 per cent abv is thus 12 parts alcohol and, in effect, 88 parts fruit juice.

The question of how much alcohol we can drink without harming ourselves in the short or long term is an impossible one to answer, but there is more or less general agreement among scientists that small amounts of alcohol are good for us, even if the only evidence of this is actuarial – the fact that mortality statistics show teetotallers live significantly shorter lives than moderate drinkers. According to the Department of Health, there are 'safe limits' to the amount of alcohol we should drink weekly. These limits are measured in units of alcohol, with a small glass of wine taken to be one unit. Men are advised that 28 units a week is the most they can drink without risk to health, and for women (whose liver function differs from that of men because of metabolic distinctions) the figure is 21 units.

If you wish to measure your consumption closely, note that a standard 75 cl bottle of wine at 12 per cent alcohol contains 9 units. A bottle of German

Moselle at 8 per cent alcohol has only 6 units, but a bottle of Australian Chardonnay at 14 per cent has 10.5.

Alentejo – Wine region of southern Portugal (immediately north of the Algarve), with a fast-improving reputation, especially for sappy, keen reds from local grape varieties including Aragones, Castelão and Trincadeira grapes.

Almansa – DO winemaking region of Spain inland from Alicante, making great-value red wines.

Alsace – France's easternmost wine-producing region lies between the Vosges Mountains and the River Rhine, with Germany beyond. These conditions make for the production of some of the world's most delicious and fascinating white wines, always sold under the name of their constituent grapes. Pinot Blanc is the most affordable – and is well worth looking out for. The 'noble' grape varieties of the region are Gewürztraminer, Muscat, Riesling and Pinot Gris and they are always made on a single-variety basis. The richest, most exotic wines are those from individual *grand cru* vineyards, which are named on the label. Some vendange tardive (late harvest) wines are made, but tend to be expensive. All the wines are sold in tall, slim green bottles known as flûtes that closely resemble those of the Mosel, and the names of producers and grape varieties are often German too, so it is widely assumed that Alsace wines are German in style, if not in nationality. But this is not the case in either particular. Alsace wines are dry and quite unique in character – and definitely French.

Amarone – Style of red wine made in Valpolicella, Italy. Specially selected grapes are held back from the harvest and stored for several months to dry them out. They are then pressed and fermented into a highly concentrated speciality dry wine. Amarone means 'bitter', describing the dry style of the flavour.

amontillado – *See* sherry.

aperitif – If a wine is thus described, I believe it will give more pleasure before a meal than with one. Crisp, low-alcohol German wines and other delicately flavoured whites (including many dry Italians) are examples.

Appellation d'Origine Contrôlée – Commonly abbreviated to AC or AOC, this is the system under which quality wines are defined in France. About a third of the country's vast annual output qualifies, and there are more than 400 distinct AC zones. The declaration of an AC on the label signifies that the wine meets standards concerning location of vineyards and wineries, grape varieties and limits on harvest per hectare, methods of cultivation and vinification, and alcohol content. Wines are inspected and tasted by state-appointed committees. The one major aspect of any given wine that an AC cannot guarantee is that you will like it – but it certainly improves the chances.

Appellation d'Origine Protégée (AOP) – Under new EU rules of 2010, already incorporated into French law, the AOC system is slowly transforming into AOP. In effect, it will mean little more than the exchange of 'controlled' with 'protected' on labels. One quirk of the new rules is that makers of AOP wines will be able to name the constituent grape variety or varieties on their labels, if they so wish.

Apulia – Anglicised name for Puglia.

Ardèche – Region of southern France to the west of the Rhône valley, home to a good vin de pays zone known as the Coteaux de L'Ardèche. Lots of decent-value reds from Syrah grapes, and some, less interesting, dry whites.

Assyrtiko – White grape variety of Greece now commonly named on dry white wines, sometimes of great quality, from the mainland and islands.

Asti – Town and major winemaking centre in Piedmont, Italy. The sparkling (spumante) sweet wines made from Moscato grapes are inexpensive and often delicious. Typical alcohol level is a modest 5 to 7 per cent.

attack – In wine tasting, the first impression made by the wine in the mouth.

Auslese – German wine-quality designation. *See* QmP.

B

Baga – Black grape variety indigenous to Portugal. Makes famously concentrated, juicy reds that get their deep colour from the grape's particularly thick skins. Look out for this name, now quite frequently quoted as the varietal on Portuguese wine labels. Often very good value for money.

balance – A big word in the vocabulary of wine tasting. Respectable wine must get two key things right: lots of fruitiness from the sweet grape juice, and plenty of acidity so the sweetness is 'balanced' with the crispness familiar in good dry whites and the dryness that marks out good reds. Some wines are noticeably 'well balanced' in that they have memorable fruitiness and the clean, satisfying 'finish' (last flavour in the mouth) that ideal acidity imparts.

Barbera – Black grape variety originally of Piedmont in Italy. Most commonly seen as Barbera d'Asti, the vigorously fruity red wine made around Asti – once better known for sweet sparkling Asti Spumante. Barbera grapes are now being grown in South America, often producing a sleeker, smoother style than at home in Italy.

Bardolino – Once fashionable, light red wine DOC of Veneto, north-west Italy. Bardolino is made principally from Corvina Veronese grapes plus Rondinella, Molinara and Negrara. Best wines are supposed to be those labelled *classico*, and *superiore* is applied to those aged a year and having at least 11.5 per cent alcohol.

Barossa Valley – Famed vineyard region north of Adelaide, Australia, produces hearty reds principally from Shiraz, Cabernet Sauvignon and Grenache grapes, plus plenty of lush white wine from Chardonnay. Also known for limey, long-lived, mineral dry whites from Riesling grapes.

barrique – Barrel in French. *En barrique* on a wine label signifies the wine has been matured in oak.

Beaujolais – Unique red wines from the southern reaches of Burgundy, France, are made from Gamay grapes. Beaujolais nouveau, now deeply unfashionable, provides a friendly introduction to the bouncy, red-fruit style of the wine, but for the authentic experience, go for Beaujolais Villages, from the region's better, northern vineyards. There are ten AC zones within this northern sector making wines under their own names. Known as the *crus*, these are Brouilly, Chénas, Chiroubles, Côte de Brouilly, Fleurie, Juliénas, Morgon, Moulin à Vent, Regnié and St Amour and produce most of the best wines of the region. Prices are higher than those for Beaujolais Villages, but by no means always justifiably so.

Beaumes de Venise – Village near Châteauneuf du Pape in France's Rhône valley, famous for sweet and alcoholic wine from Muscat grapes. Delicious, grapey wines. A small number of growers also make strong (sometimes rather tough) red wines under the village name.

Beaune – One of the two winemaking centres (the other is Nuits St Georges) at the heart of Burgundy in France. Three of the region's humbler appellations take the name of the town: Côtes de Beaune, Côtes de Beaune Villages and Hautes Côtes de Beaune. Wines made under these ACs are often, but by no means always, good value for money.

berry fruit – Some red wines deliver a burst of flavour in the mouth that corresponds to biting into a newly picked berry – strawberry, blackberry, etc. So a wine described as having berry fruit (by this writer, anyway) has freshness, liveliness, immediate appeal.

bianco – White wine, Italy.

Bical – White grape variety principally of Dão region of northern Portugal. Not usually identified on labels, because most of it goes into inexpensive sparkling wines. Can make still wines of very refreshing crispness.

biodynamics – A cultivation method taking the organic approach several steps further. Biodynamic winemakers plant and tend their vineyards according to a date and time calendar 'in harmony' with the movements of the planets. Some of France's best-known wine estates subscribe, and many more are going that way. It might all sound bonkers, but it's salutary to learn that biodynamics is based on principles first described by a very eminent man, the Austrian educationist Rudolph Steiner. He's lately been in the news for having written, in 1919, that farmers crazy enough to feed animal products to cattle would drive the livestock 'mad'.

bite – In wine tasting, the impression on the palate of a wine with plenty of acidity and, often, tannin.

blanc – White wine, France.

blanc de blancs – White wine from white grapes, France. May seem to be stating the obvious, but some white wines (e.g. champagne) are made, partially or entirely, from black grapes.

blanc de noirs – White wine from black grapes, France. Usually sparkling (especially champagne) made from black Pinot Meunier and Pinot Noir grapes, with no Chardonnay or other white varieties.

blanco – White wine, Spain and Portugal.

Blauer Zweigelt – Black grape variety of Austria, making a large proportion of the country's red wines, some of excellent quality.

Bobal – Black grape variety mostly of south-eastern Spain. Thick skin is good for colour and juice contributes acidity to blends.

bodega – In Spain, a wine producer or wine shop.

Bonarda – Black grape variety of northern Italy. Now more widely planted in Argentina, where it makes rather elegant red wines, often representing great value.

botrytis – Full name, *botrytis cinerea*, is that of a beneficent fungus that can attack ripe grape bunches late in the season, shrivelling the berries to a gruesome-looking mess, which yields concentrated juice of prized sweetness. Cheerfully known as 'noble rot', this fungus is actively encouraged by winemakers in regions as diverse as Sauternes (in Bordeaux), Monbazillac (in Bergerac), the Rhine and Mosel valleys, Hungary's Tokaji region and South Australia to make ambrosial dessert wines.

bouncy – The feel in the mouth of a red wine with young, juicy fruitiness. Good Beaujolais is bouncy, as are many north-west-Italian wines from Barbera and Dolcetto grapes.

Bourgogne Grand Ordinaire – Appellation of France's Burgundy region for 'ordinary' red and rosé wines from either Gamay or Pinot Noir grapes, or both, and whites from Chardonnay or Aligoté. Some good-value wines, especially from the Buxy co-operative in the southern Chalonnais area.

Bourgueil – Appellation of Loire Valley, France. Long-lived red wines from Cabernet Franc grapes.

briary – In wine tasting, associated with the flavours of fruit from prickly bushes such as blackberries.

brûlé – Pleasant burnt-toffee taste or smell, as in crème brûlée.

brut – Driest style of sparkling wine. Originally French, for very dry champagnes specially developed for the British market, but now used for sparkling wines from all round the world.

Buzet – Little-seen AC of south-west France overshadowed by Bordeaux but producing some characterful ripe reds.

C

Cabardès – Recent AC (1998) for red and rosé wines from area north of Carcassonne, Aude, France. Principally Cabernet Sauvignon and Merlot grapes.

Cabernet Franc – Black grape variety originally of France. It makes the light-bodied and keenly-edged red wines of the Loire Valley – such as Chinon and Saumur. And it is much grown in Bordeaux, especially in the appellation of St Emilion. Also now planted in Argentina, Australia and North America. Wines, especially in the Loire, are characterised by a leafy, sappy style and bold fruitiness. Most are best enjoyed young.

Cabernet Sauvignon – Black (or, rather, blue) grape variety now grown in virtually every wine-producing nation. When perfectly ripened, the grapes are smaller than many other varieties and have particularly thick skins. This means that when pressed, Cabernet grapes have a high proportion of skin to juice – and that makes for wine with lots of colour and tannin. In Bordeaux, the grape's traditional home, the grandest Cabernet-based wines have always been known as *vins de garde* (wines to keep) because they take years, even decades, to evolve as the effect of all that skin extraction preserves the fruit all the way to magnificent maturity. But in today's impatient world, these grapes are exploited in modern winemaking techniques to produce the sublime flavours of mature Cabernet without having to hang around for lengthy periods awaiting maturation. While there's nothing like a fine, ten-year-old claret (and nothing quite as expensive), there are many excellent Cabernets from around the world that amply illustrate this grape's characteristics. Classic smells and flavours include blackcurrants, cedar wood, chocolate, tobacco – even violets.

Cahors – An AC of the Lot Valley in south-west France once famous for 'black wine'. This was a curious concoction of straightforward wine mixed with a soupy must, made by boiling up new-pressed juice to concentrate it (through evaporation) before fermentation. The myth is still perpetuated that Cahors wine continues to be made in this way, but production on this basis actually ceased 150 years ago. Cahors today is no stronger, or blacker, than the wines of neighbouring appellations.

Cairanne – Village of the appellation collectively known as the Côtes du Rhône in southern France. Cairanne is one of several villages entitled to put their name on the labels of wines made within their AC boundary, and the appearance of this name is quite reliably an indicator of a very good wine indeed.

Calatayud – DO (quality wine zone) near Zaragoza in the Aragon region of northern Spain where they're making some astonishingly good wines at bargain prices, mainly reds from Garnacha and Tempranillo grapes. These are the varieties that go into the light and oaky wines of Rioja, but in Calatayud, the wines are dark, dense and decidedly different.

Cannonau – Black grape native to Sardinia by name, but in fact the same variety as the ubiquitous Grenache of France (and Garnacha of Spain).

cantina sociale – *See* Co-op.

Carignan – Black grape variety of Mediterranean France. It is rarely identified on labels, but is a major constituent of wines from the southern Rhône and Languedoc-Roussillon regions. Known as Carignano in Italy and Cariñena in Spain.

Cariñena – A region of north-east Spain, south of Navarra, known for substantial reds, as well as the Spanish name for the Carignan grape (*qv*).

Carmenère – Black grape variety once widely grown in Bordeaux but abandoned due to cultivation problems. Lately revived in South America where it is producing fine wines, sometimes with echoes of Bordeaux.

cassis – As a tasting note, signifies a wine that has a noticeable blackcurrant-concentrate flavour or smell. Much associated with the Cabernet Sauvignon grape.

Castelao – Portuguese black grape variety. Same as Periquita.

Catarratto – White grape variety of Sicily. In skilled hands it can make anything from keen, green-fruit dry whites to lush, oaked super-ripe styles. Also used for Marsala.

cat's pee – In tasting notes, a mildly jocular reference to a certain style of Sauvignon Blanc wine.

cava – The sparkling wine of Spain. Most originates in Catalonia, but the Denominación de Origen (DO) guarantee of authenticity is open to producers in many regions of the country. Much cava is very reasonably priced even though it is made by the same method as champagne – second fermentation in bottle, known in Spain as the *método clásico*.

CdR – Côtes du Rhône.

Cépage – Grape variety, French. 'Cépage Merlot' on a label simply means the wine is made largely or exclusively from Merlot grapes.

Chablis – Northernmost AC of France's Burgundy region. Its dry white wines from Chardonnay grapes are known for their fresh and steely style, but the best wines also age very gracefully into complex classics.

Chambourcin – Sounds like a cream cheese but it's a relatively modern (1963) French hybrid black grape that makes some good non-appellation lightweight-but-concentrated reds in the Loire Valley and now some heftier versions in Australia.

Chardonnay – The world's most popular grape variety. Said to originate from the village of Chardonnay in the Mâconnais region of southern Burgundy, the vine is now planted in every wine-producing nation. Wines are commonly characterised by generous colour and sweet-apple smell, but styles range from lean and sharp to opulently rich. Australia started the craze for oaked Chardonnay, the gold-coloured, super-ripe, buttery 'upfront' wines that are a caricature of lavish and outrageously expensive burgundies such as Meursault and Puligny-Montrachet. Rich to the point of egginess, these Aussie pretenders are now giving way to a sleeker, more minerally style with much less oak presence – if any at all. California and Chile, New Zealand and South Africa are competing hard to imitate the Burgundian style, and Australia's success in doing so.

Châteauneuf du Pape – Famed appellation centred on a picturesque village of the southern Rhône valley in France where in the 1320s French Pope Clement V had a splendid new château built for himself as a country retreat amidst his vineyards. The red wines of the AC, which can be made from 13 different grape varieties but principally Grenache, Syrah and Mourvèdre, are regarded as the best of the southern Rhône and have become rather expensive – but they can be sensationally good. Expensive white wines are also made.

Chenin Blanc – White grape variety of the Loire Valley, France. Now also grown farther afield, especially in South Africa. Makes dry, soft white wines and also rich, sweet styles. Sadly, many low-cost Chenin wines are bland and uninteresting.

cherry – In wine tasting, either a pale red colour or, more commonly, a smell or flavour akin to the sun-warmed, bursting sweet ripeness of cherries. Many Italian wines, from lightweights such as Bardolino and Valpolicella to serious Chianti, have this character. 'Black cherry' as a description is often used of Merlot wines – meaning they are sweet but have a firmness associated with the thicker skins of black cherries.

Cinsault – Black grape variety of southern France, where it is invariably blended with others in wines of all qualities ranging from vin de pays to the pricy reds of Châteauneuf du Pape. Also much planted in South Africa. The effect in wine is to add keen aromas (sometimes compared with turpentine!) and softness to the blend. The name is often spelt Cinsaut.

Clape, La – A small *cru* (defined quality-vineyard area) within the Coteaux du Languedoc where the growers make some seriously delicious red wines, mainly from Carignan, Grenache and Syrah grapes. A name worth looking out for on labels from the region.

claret – The red wine of Bordeaux, France. It comes from Latin *clarus*, meaning 'clear', recalling a time when the red wines of the region were much lighter in colour than they are now.

clarete – On Spanish labels indicates a pale-coloured red wine. Tinto signifies a deeper hue.

classed growth – English translation of French *cru classé* describes a group of 60 individual wine estates in the Médoc district of Bordeaux, which in 1855 were granted this new status on the basis that their wines were the most expensive at that time. The classification was a promotional wheeze to attract attention to the Bordeaux stand at that year's Great Exhibition in Paris. Amazingly, all of the 60 wines concerned are still in production and most still occupy more or less their original places in the pecking order price-wise. The league was divided up into five divisions from *Premier Grand Cru Classé* (just four wines originally, with one promoted in 1971 – the only change ever made to the classification) to *Cinquième Grand Cru Classé*. Other regions of Bordeaux, notably Graves and St Emilion, have since imitated Médoc and introduced their own rankings of *cru classé* estates.

classic – An overused term in every respect – wine descriptions being no exception. In this book, the word is used to describe a very good wine of its type. So, a 'classic' Cabernet Sauvignon is one that is recognisably and admirably characteristic of that grape.

Classico – Under Italy's wine laws, this word appended to the name of a DOC zone has an important significance. The classico wines of the region can only be made from vineyards lying in the best-rated areas, and wines thus labelled (e.g. Chianti Classico, Soave Classico, Valpolicella Classico) can be reliably counted on to be a cut above the rest.

Colombard – White grape variety of southern France. Once employed almost entirely for making the wine that is distilled for armagnac and cognac brandies, but lately restored to varietal prominence in the Vin de Pays des Côtes de Gascogne where high-tech wineries turn it into a fresh and crisp, if unchallenging, dry wine at a budget price. But beware, cheap Colombard (especially from South Africa) can still be very dull.

Conca de Barbera – Winemaking region of Catalonia, Spain.

co-op – Very many of France's good-quality, inexpensive wines are made by co-operatives. These are wine-producing factories whose members, and joint-owners, are local *vignerons* (vine growers). Each year they sell their harvests to the co-op for turning into branded wines. In Italy, co-op wines can be identified by the words *Cantina Sociale* on the label and in Germany by the term *Winzergenossenschaft*.

Corbières – A name to look out for. It's an AC of France's Midi (deep south) and produces countless robust reds and a few interesting whites, often at bargain prices.

Cortese – White grape variety of Piedmont, Italy. At its best, makes amazingly delicious, keenly brisk and fascinating wines, including those of the Gavi DOCG. Worth seeking out.

Costières de Nîmes – Until 1989, this AC of southern France was known as the Costières de Gard. It forms a buffer between the southern Rhône and Languedoc-Roussillon regions, and makes wines from broadly the same range of grape varieties. It's a name to look out for, the best red wines being notable for their concentration of colour and fruit, with the earthy-spiciness of the better Rhône wines and a likeable liquorice note. A few good white wines, too, and even a decent rosé or two.

Côte – In French, it simply means a side, or slope, of a hill. The implication in wine terms is that the grapes come from a vineyard ideally situated for maximum sunlight, good drainage and the unique soil conditions prevailing on the hill in question. It's fair enough to claim that vines grown on slopes might get more sunlight than those grown on the flat, but there is no guarantee whatsoever that any wine labelled 'Côtes du' this or that is made from grapes grown on a hillside anyway. Côtes du Rhône wines are a case in point. Many 'Côtes' wines come from entirely level vineyards and it is worth remembering that many of the vineyards of Bordeaux, producing most of the world's priciest wines, are little short of prairie-flat. The quality factor is determined much more significantly by the weather and the talents of the winemaker.

Côtes de Blaye – Appellation Contrôlée zone of Bordeaux on the right bank of the River Gironde, opposite the more prestigious Médoc zone of the left bank. Best-rated vineyards qualify for the AC Premières Côtes de Blaye. A couple of centuries ago, Blaye (pronounced 'bligh') was the grander of the two, and even today makes some wines that compete well for quality, and at a fraction of the price of wines from its more fashionable rival across the water.

Côtes de Bourg – AC neighbouring Côtes de Blaye, making red wines of fast-improving quality and value.

Côtes du Luberon – Appellation Contrôlée zone of Provence in south-east France. Wines, mostly red, are similar in style to Côtes du Rhône.

Côtes du Rhône – One of the biggest and best-known appellations of southeast France, covering an area roughly defined by the southern reaches of the valley of the River Rhône. Long notorious for cheap and execrable reds, the Côtes du Rhône AC has lately achieved remarkable improvements in quality at all points along the price scale. Lots of brilliant-value warm and spicy reds, principally from Grenache and Syrah grapes. There are also some white and rosé wines.

Côtes du Rhône Villages – Appellation within the larger Côtes du Rhône AC for wine of supposed superiority made in a number of zones associated with a long list of nominated individual villages.

Côtes du Roussillon – Huge appellation of south-west France known for strong, dark, peppery reds often offering very decent value.

Côtes du Roussillon Villages – Appellation for superior wines from a number of nominated locations within the larger Roussillon AC. Some of these village wines can be of exceptional quality and value.

crianza – Means 'nursery' in Spanish. On Rioja and Navarra wines, the designation signifies a wine that has been nursed through a maturing period of at least a year in oak casks and a further six months in bottle before being released for sale.

cru – A word that crops up with confusing regularity on French wine labels. It means 'the growing' or 'the making' of a wine and asserts that the wine concerned is from a specific vineyard. Under the Appellation Contrôlée rules, countless *crus* are classified in various hierarchical ranks. Hundreds of individual vineyards are described as *premier cru* or *grand cru* in the classic wine regions of Alsace, Bordeaux, Burgundy and Champagne. The common denominator is that the wine can be counted on to be enormously expensive. On humbler wines, the use of the word *cru* tends to be mere decoration.

cru classé – *See* classed growth.

cuve – A vat for wine. French.

cuvée – French for the wine in a cuve, or vat. The word is much used on labels to imply that the wine is from just one vat, and thus of unique, unblended character. Première cuvée is supposedly the best wine from a given pressing because the grapes have had only the initial, gentle squashing to extract the free-run juice. Subsequent cuvées will have been from harsher pressings, grinding the grape pulp to extract the last drop of juice.

D

Dão – Major wine-producing region of northern Portugal now turning out much more interesting reds than it used to – worth looking out for anything made by mega-producer Sogrape.

demi sec – 'Half-dry' style of French (and some other) wines. Beware. It can mean anything from off-dry to cloyingly sweet.

DO – Denominación de Origen, Spain's wine-regulating scheme, similar to France's AC, but older – the first DO region was Rioja, from 1926. DO wines are Spain's best, accounting for a third of the nation's annual production.

DOC – Stands for Denominazione di Origine Controllata, Italy's equivalent of France's AC. The wines are made according to the stipulations of each of the system's 300-plus denominated zones of origin, along with a further 70-odd zones, which enjoy the superior classification of DOCG (DOC with *e Garantita* – guaranteed – appended).

Durif – Rare black grape variety mostly of California, where it is also known as Petite Sirah, but with some plantings in Australia.

E

earthy – A tricky word in the wine vocabulary. In this book, its use is meant to be complimentary. It indicates that the wine somehow suggests the soil the grapes were grown in, even (perhaps a shade too poetically) the landscape in which the vineyards lie. The amazing-value red wines of the torrid, volcanic southernmost regions of Italy are often described as earthy. This is an association with the pleasantly 'scorched' back-flavour in wines made from the ultra-ripe harvests of this near-sub-tropical part of the world.

edge – A wine with edge is one with evident (although not excessive) acidity.

élevé – 'Brought up' in French. Much used on wine labels where the wine has been matured (brought up) in oak barrels, *élevé en fûts de chêne*, to give it extra dimensions.

Entre Deux Mers – Meaning 'between two seas', it's a region lying between the Dordogne and Garonne rivers of Bordeaux, now mainly known for dry white wines from Sauvignon and Semillon grapes.

Estremadura – Wine-producing region occupying Portugal's coastal area north of Lisbon. Lots of interesting wines from indigenous grape varieties, usually at bargain prices. If a label mentions Estremadura, it is a safe rule that there might be something good within.

F

Falanghina – Revived ancient grape variety of southern Italy now making some superbly fresh and tangy white wines.

Faugères – AC of the Languedoc in south-west France. Source of many hearty, economic reds.

Feteasca – White grape variety widely grown in Romania. Name means 'maiden's grape' and the wine tends to be soft and slightly sweet.

Fiano – White grape variety of the Campania of southern Italy and Sicily, lately revived. It is said to have been cultivated by the ancient Romans for a wine called Apianum.

finish – The last flavour lingering in the mouth after wine has been swallowed.

fino – Pale and very dry style of sherry. You drink it thoroughly chilled – and you don't keep it any longer after opening than other dry white wines. Needs to be fresh to be at its best.

Fitou – One of the first 'designer' wines, it's an appellation in France's Languedoc region, where production is dominated by one huge co-operative, the Vignerons de Mont Tauch. Back in the 1970s, this co-op paid a corporate-image company to come up with a Fitou logo and label-design style, and the wines have prospered ever since. And it's not just packaging – Fitou at all price levels can be very good value, especially from the Mont Tauch co-op.

flabby – Fun word describing a wine that tastes dilute or watery, with insufficient acidity.

fruit – In tasting terms, the fruit is the greater part of the overall flavour of a wine. The wine is (or should be) after all, composed entirely of fruit.

G

Gamay – The black grape that makes all red Beaujolais and some ordinary burgundy. It is a pretty safe rule to avoid Gamay wines from any other region, but there are exceptions.

Garganega – White grape variety of the Veneto region of north-east Italy. Best known as the principal ingredient of Soave, but occasionally included in varietal blends and mentioned as such on labels. Correctly pronounced 'gar-GAN-iga'.

Garnacha – Spanish black grape variety synonymous with Grenache of France. It is blended with Tempranillo to make the red wines of Rioja and Navarra, and is now quite widely cultivated elsewhere in Spain to make grippingly fruity varietals.

garrigue – Arid land of France's deep south giving its name to a style of red wine that notionally evokes the herby, heated, peppery flavours associated with such a landscape. A tricky metaphor!

Gavi – DOCG for dry but rich white wine from Cortese grapes in Piedmont, north-west Italy. Trendy Gavi di Gavi wines tend to be enjoyably lush, but are rather expensive.

Gewürztraminer – One of the great grape varieties of Alsace, France. At their best, the wines are perfumed with lychees and are richly, spicily fruity, yet quite dry. Gewürztraminer from Alsace is almost always relatively expensive, but the grape is also grown with some success in Eastern Europe, Germany, Italy, New Zealand and South America, and sold at more approachable prices. Pronounced 'ge-VOORTS-traminner'.

Givry – AC for red and white wines in the Côte Chalonnaise sub-region of Burgundy. Source of some wonderfully natural-tasting reds that might be lighter than those of the more prestigious Côte d'Or to the north, but have great merits of their own. Relatively, the wines are often underpriced.

Glera – alternative name for Prosecco grape of northern Italy.

Graciano – Black grape variety of Spain that is one of the minor constituents of Rioja. Better known in its own right in Australia where it can make dense, spicy, long-lived red wines.

green – I don't often use this in the pejorative. Green, to me, is a likeable degree of freshness, especially in Sauvignon Blanc wines.

Grenache – The mainstay of the wines of the southern Rhône Valley in France. Grenache is usually the greater part of the mix in Côtes du Rhône reds and is widely planted right across the neighbouring Languedoc-Roussillon region. It's a big-cropping variety that thrives even in the hottest climates and is really a blending grape – most commonly with Syrah, the noble variety of the northern Rhône. Few French wines are labelled with its name, but the grape has caught on in Australia in a big way and it is now becoming a familiar varietal, known for strong, dark liquorous reds. Grenache is the French name for what is originally a Spanish variety, Garnacha.

Grillo – White grape of Sicily said to be among the island's oldest indigenous varieties, pre-dating the arrival of the Greeks in 600 BC. Much used for fortified Marsala, it has lately been revived for interesting, aromatic dry table wines.

grip – In wine-tasting terminology, the sensation in the mouth produced by a wine that has a healthy quantity of tannin in it. A wine with grip is a good wine. A wine with too much tannin, or which is still too young (the tannin hasn't 'softened' with age) is not described as having grip, but as mouth-puckering – or simply undrinkable.

Grolleau – Black grape variety of the Loire Valley principally cultivated for Rosé d'Anjou.

Grüner Veltliner – The 'national' white-wine grape of Austria. In the past it made mostly soft, German-style everyday wines, but now is behind some excellent dry styles, too.

H

halbtrocken – 'Half-dry' in Germany's wine vocabulary. A reassurance that the wine is not some ghastly sugared Liebfraumilch-style confection.

hock – The wine of Germany's Rhine river valleys. Traditionally, but no longer consistently, it comes in brown bottles, as distinct from the wine of the Mosel river valleys – which comes in green ones.

I

Indicazione Geografica Tipica – Italy's recently instituted wine-quality designation, broadly equivalent to France's vin de pays. The label has to state the geographical location of the vineyard and will often (but not always) state the principal grape varieties from which the wine is made.

Indication Géographique Protégée (IGP) – Introduced to France in 2010 under new EU-wide wine-designation rules, IGP covers the wines hitherto known as Vins de Pays. Some wines are already being labelled IGP, but established Vins de Pays producers are unlikely to redesignate their products in a hurry, and are not obliged to do so. Some will abbreviate, so, for example, Vin de Pays d'Oc shortens to Pays d'Oc.

J

jammy – The 'sweetness' in dry red wines is supposed to evoke ripeness rather than sugariness. Sometimes, flavours include a sweetness reminiscent of jam. Usually a fault in the winemaking technique.

joven – Young wine, Spanish. In regions such as Rioja, vino joven is a synonym for sin crianza, which means 'without ageing' in cask or bottle.

K

Kabinett – Under Germany's bewildering wine-quality rules, this is a classification of a top-quality (QmP) wine. Expect a keen, dry, racy style. The name comes from the cabinet or cupboard in which winemakers traditionally kept their most treasured bottles.

Kekfrankos – Black grape variety of Hungary, particularly the Sopron region, which makes some of the country's more interesting red wines, characterised by colour and spiciness. Same variety as Austria's Blaufrankisch.

L

Ladoix – Unfashionable AC at northern edge of Côtes de Beaune makes some of Burgundy's true bargain reds. A name to look out for.

Lambrusco – The name is that of a black grape variety widely grown across northern Italy. True Lambrusco wine is red, dry and very slightly sparkling, but from the 1980s Britain has been deluged with a strange, sweet manifestation of the style, which has done little to enhance the good name of the original. Good Lambrusco is delicious and fun, but in this country now very hard to find.

Languedoc-Roussillon – Vast area of southern France, including the country's south-west Mediterranean region. The source, now, of many great-value wines from countless ACs and vin de pays zones.

lees – The detritus of the winemaking process that collects in the bottom of the vat or cask. Wines left for extended periods on the lees can acquire extra dimensions of flavour, in particular a 'leesy' creaminess.

legs – The liquid residue left clinging to the sides of the glass after wine has been swirled. The persistence of the legs is an indicator of the weight of alcohol. Also known as 'tears'.

lieu dit – This is starting to appear on French wine labels. It translates as an 'agreed place' and is an area of vineyard defined as of particular character or merit, but not classified under wine law. Usually, the lieu dit's name is stated, with the implication that the wine in question has special value.

liquorice – The pungent slightly burnt flavours of this once-fashionable confection are detectable in some wines made from very ripe grapes, for example, the Malbec harvested in Argentina and several varieties grown in the very hot vineyards of southernmost Italy. A close synonym is 'tarry'. This characteristic is by no means a fault in red wine, unless very dominant, but it can make for a challenging flavour that might not appeal to all tastes.

liquorous – Wines of great weight and glyceriney texture (evidenced by the 'legs', or 'tears', which cling to the glass after the wine has been swirled) are always noteworthy. The connection with liquor is drawn in respect of the feel of the wine in the mouth, rather than with the higher alcoholic strength of spirits.

Lugana – DOC of Lombardy, Italy known for a dry white wine that is often of real distinction – rich, almondy stuff from the ubiquitous Trebbiano grape.

M

Macabeo – One of the main grapes used for cava, the sparkling wine of Spain. It is the same grape as Viura.

Mâcon – Town and collective appellation of southern Burgundy, France. Lightweight white wines from Chardonnay grapes and similarly light reds from Pinot Noir and some Gamay. The better ones, and the ones exported, have the AC Mâcon-Villages and there are individual village wines with their own ACs including Mâcon-Clessé, Mâcon-Viré and Mâcon-Lugny.

Malbec – Black grape variety grown on a small scale in Bordeaux, and the mainstay of the wines of Cahors in France's Dordogne region under the name Cot. Now much better known for producing big butch reds in Argentina.

Manzanilla – Pale, very dry sherry of Sanlucar de Barrameda, a resort town on the Bay of Cadiz in Spain. Manzanilla is proud to be distinct from the pale, very dry fino sherry of the main producing town of Jerez de la Frontera an hour's drive inland. Drink it chilled and fresh – it goes downhill in an opened bottle after just a few days, even if kept (as it should be) in the fridge.

Margaret River – Vineyard region of Western Australia regarded as ideal for grape varieties including Cabernet Sauvignon. It has a relatively cool climate and a reputation for making sophisticated wines, both red and white.

Marlborough – Best-known vineyard region of New Zealand's South Island has a cool climate and a name for brisk but cerebral Sauvignon Blanc and Chardonnay wines.

Marsanne – White grape variety of the northern Rhône Valley and, increasingly, of the wider south of France. It's known for making well-coloured wines with heady aroma and fruit.

Mataro – Black grape variety of Australia. It's the same as the Mourvèdre of France and Monastrell of Spain.

McLaren Vale – Vineyard region south of Adelaide in south-east Australia. Known for blockbuster Shiraz (and Chardonnay) that can be of great balance and quality from winemakers who keep the ripeness under control.

meaty – Weighty, rich red wine style.

Mendoza – The region to watch in Argentina. Lying to the east of the Andes mountains, just about opposite the best vineyards of Chile on the other side, Mendoza accounts for the bulk of Argentine wine production, with quality improving fast.

Merlot – One of the great black wine grapes of Bordeaux, and now grown all over the world. The name is said to derive from the French merle, meaning a blackbird. Characteristics of Merlot-based wines attract descriptions such as 'plummy' and 'plump' with black-cherry aroma. The grapes are larger than most, and thus have less skin in proportion to their flesh. This means the resulting wines have less tannin than wines from smaller-berry varieties such as Cabernet Sauvignon, and are therefore, in the Bordeaux context at least, more suitable for drinking while still relatively young.

middle palate – In wine tasting, the impression given by the wine when it is held in the mouth.

Midi – Catch-all term for the deep south of France west of the Rhône Valley.

mineral – Good dry white wines can have a crispness and freshness that somehow evokes this word. Purity of flavour is a key.

Minervois – AC for (mostly) red wines from vineyards around the town of Minerve in the Languedoc-Roussillon region of France. Often good value. The new Minervois La Livinière AC – a sort of Minervois *Grand Cru* – is host to some great estates including Château Maris and Vignobles Lorgeril.

Monastrell – Black grape variety of Spain, widely planted in Mediterranean regions for inexpensive wines notable for their high alcohol and toughness – though they can mature into excellent, soft reds. The variety is known in France as Mourvèdre and in Australia as Mataro.

Monbazillac – AC for sweet, dessert wines within the wider appellation of Bergerac in south-west France. Made from the same grape varieties (principally Sauvignon and Semillon) that go into the much costlier counterpart wines of Barsac and Sauternes near Bordeaux, these stickies from botrytis-affected, late-harvested grapes can be delicious and good value for money.

Montalcino – Hill town of Tuscany, Italy, and a DOCG for strong and very long-lived red wines from Brunello grapes. The wines are mostly very expensive. Rosso di Montalcino, a DOC for the humbler wines of the zone, is often a good buy.

Montepulciano – Black grape variety of Italy. Best known in Montepulciano d'Abruzzo, the juicy, purply-black and bramble-fruited red of the Abruzzi region midway down Italy's Adriatic side. Also the grape in the rightly popular hearty reds of Rosso Conero from around Ancona in the Marches. Not to be confused with the hill town of Montepulciano in Tuscany, famous for expensive Vino Nobile di Montepulciano wine.

morello – Lots of red wines have smells and flavours redolent of cherries. Morello cherries, among the darkest coloured and sweetest of all varieties and the preferred choice of cherry-brandy producers, have a distinct sweetness resembled by some wines made from Merlot grapes. A morello whiff or taste is generally very welcome.

Moscatel – Spanish Muscat.

Moscato – *See* Muscat.

Moselle – The wine of Germany's Mosel river valleys, collectively known for winemaking purposes as Mosel-Saar-Ruwer. The wine always comes in slim, green bottles, as distinct from the brown bottles traditionally, but no longer exclusively, employed for Rhine wines.

Mourvèdre – Widely planted black grape variety of southern France. It's an ingredient in many of the wines of Provence, the Rhône and Languedoc, including the ubiquitous Vin de Pays d'Oc. It's a hot-climate vine and the wine is usually blended with other varieties to give sweet aromas and 'backbone' to the mix. Known as Mataro in Australia and Monastrell in Spain.

Muscadet – One of France's most familiar everyday whites, made from a grape called the Melon or Melon de Bourgogne. It comes from vineyards at the estuarial end of the River Loire, and has a sea-breezy freshness about it. The better wines are reckoned to be those from the vineyards in the Sèvre et Maine region, and many are made sur lie – 'on the lees' – meaning that the wine is left in contact with the yeasty deposit of its fermentation until just before bottling, in an endeavour to add interest to what can sometimes be an acidic and fruitless style.

Muscat – Grape variety with origins in ancient Greece, and still grown widely among the Aegean islands for the production of sweet white wines. Muscats are the wines that taste more like grape juice than any other – but the high sugar levels ensure they are also among the most alcoholic of wines, too. Known as Moscato in Italy, the grape is much used for making sweet sparkling wines, as in Asti Spumante or Moscato d'Asti. There are several appellations in south-west France for inexpensive Muscats made rather like port, part-fermented before the addition of grape alcohol to halt the conversion of sugar into alcohol, creating a sweet and heady vin doux naturel. Dry Muscat wines, when well made, have a delicious sweet aroma but a refreshing, light touch with flavours reminiscent variously of orange blossom, wood smoke and grapefruit.

must – New-pressed grape juice prior to fermentation.

N

Navarra – DO wine-producing region of northern Spain adjacent to, and overshadowed by, Rioja. Navarra's wines can be startlingly akin to their neighbouring rivals, and sometimes rather better value for money.

négociant – In France, a dealer-producer who buys wines from growers and matures and/or blends them for sale under his or her own label. Purists can be a bit sniffy about these entrepreneurs, claiming that only the vine-grower with his or her own winemaking set-up can make truly authentic stuff, but the truth is that many of the best wines of France are négociant-produced – especially at the humbler end of the price scale. Négociants are often identified on wine labels as négociant-éleveur (literally 'dealer-bringer-up') and meaning that the wine has been matured, blended and bottled by the party in question.

Negroamaro – Black grape variety mainly of Apulia, the fast-improving wine region of south-east Italy. Dense, earthy red wines with ageing potential and plenty of alcohol. The grape behind Copertino.

Nerello Mascalese – Black grape of Sicily making light, flavoursome and alcoholic reds.

Nero d'Avola – Black grape variety of Sicily and southern Italy. It makes deep-coloured wines that, given half a chance, can develop intensity and richness with age.

non-vintage – A wine is described as such when it has been blended from the harvests of more than one year. A non-vintage wine is not necessarily an inferior one, but under quality-control regulations around the world, still table wines most usually derive solely from one year's grape crop to qualify for appellation status. Champagnes and sparkling wines are mostly blended from several vintages, as are fortified wines, such as basic port and sherry.

nose – In the vocabulary of the wine-taster, the nose is the scent of a wine. Sounds a bit dotty, but it makes a sensible enough alternative to the rather bald 'smell'. The use of the word 'perfume' implies that the wine smells particularly good. 'Aroma' is used specifically to describe a wine that smells as it should, as in 'this burgundy has the authentic strawberry-raspberry aroma of Pinot Noir'.

O

oak – Most of the world's costliest wines are matured in new or nearly new oak barrels, giving additional opulence of flavour. Of late, many cheaper wines have been getting the oak treatment, too, in older, cheaper casks, or simply by having sacks of oak chippings poured into their steel or fibreglass holding tanks. 'Oak aged' on a label is likely to indicate the latter treatments. But the overtly oaked wines of Australia have in some cases been so overdone that there is now a reactive trend whereby some producers proclaim their wines – particularly Chardonnays – as 'unoaked' on the label, thereby asserting that the flavours are more naturally achieved.

Oltrepo Pavese – Wine-producing zone of Piedmont, north-west Italy. The name means 'south of Pavia across the [river] Po' and the wines, both white and red, can be excellent quality and value for money.

organic wine – As in other sectors of the food industry, demand for organically made wine is – or appears to be – growing. As a rule, a wine qualifies as organic if it comes entirely from grapes grown in vineyards cultivated without the use of synthetic materials, and made in a winery where chemical treatments or additives are shunned with similar vigour. In fact, there are plenty of winemakers in the world using organic methods, but who disdain to label their bottles as such. Wines proclaiming their organic status used to carry the same sort of premium as their counterparts round the corner in the fruit, vegetable and meat aisles. But organic viticulture is now commonplace and there seems little price impact. There is no single worldwide (or even Europe-wide) standard for organic food or wine, so you pretty much have to take the producer's word for it.

P

Pasqua – One of the biggest and, it should be said, best wine producers of the Veneto region of north-west Italy.

Passetoutgrains – Bourgogne passetoutgrains is a generic appellation of the Burgundy region, France. The word loosely means 'any grapes allowed' and is supposed specifically to designate a red wine made with Gamay grapes as well as Burgundy's principal black variety, Pinot Noir, in a ratio of two parts Gamay to one of Pinot. The wine is usually relatively inexpensive, and relatively uninteresting, too.

Periquita – Black grape variety of southern Portugal. Makes rather exotic spicy reds. Name means 'parrot'.

Petit Verdot – Black grape variety of Bordeaux used to give additional colour, density and spiciness to Cabernet Sauvignon-dominated blends. Mostly a minority player at home, but in Australia and California it is grown as the principal variety for some big hearty reds of real character.

petrol – When white wines from certain grapes, especially Riesling, are allowed to age in the bottle for longer than a year or two, they can take on a spirity aroma reminiscent of petrol or diesel. In grand mature German wines, this is considered a very good thing.

Picpoul – Grape variety of southern France. Best known in Picpoul de Pinet, a dry white from near Carcassonne in the Languedoc. The name Picpoul means 'stings the lips' – referring to the natural high acidity of the juice.

Piemonte – North-western province of Italy, which we call Piedmont, known for the spumante wines of the town of Asti, plus expensive

Barbaresco and Barolo and better-value varietal red wines from Barbera and Dolcetto grapes.

Pinotage – South Africa's own black grape variety. Makes red wines ranging from light and juicy to dark, strong and long-lived. It's a cross between Pinot Noir and a grape the South Africans used to call Hermitage (thus the portmanteau name) but turns out to have been Cinsault.

Pinot Blanc – White grape variety principally of Alsace, France. Florally perfumed, exotically fruity dry white wines.

Pinot Grigio – White grape variety of northern Italy. Wines bearing its name are perplexingly fashionable. Good examples have an interesting smoky-pungent aroma and keen, slaking fruit. But most are dull. Originally French, it is at its best in the lushly exotic Pinot Gris wines of Alsace and is also successfully cultivated in Germany and New Zealand.

Pinot Noir – The great black grape of Burgundy, France. It makes all the region's fabulously expensive red wines. Notoriously difficult to grow in warmer climates, it is nevertheless cultivated by countless intrepid winemakers in the New World intent on reproducing the magic appeal of red burgundy. California and New Zealand have come closest, but rarely at prices much below those for the real thing. Some Chilean Pinot Noirs are inexpensive and worth trying.

Pouilly Fuissé – Village and AC of the Mâconnais region of southern Burgundy in France. Dry white wines from Chardonnay grapes. Wines are among the highest rated of the Mâconnais.

Pouilly Fumé – Village and AC of the Loire Valley in France. Dry white wines from Sauvignon Blanc grapes. Similar 'pebbly', 'grassy' or even 'gooseberry' style to neighbouring AC Sancerre. The notion put about by some enthusiasts that Pouilly Fumé is 'smoky' is surely nothing more than word association with the name.

Primitivo – Black grape variety of southern Italy, especially the region of Puglia. Named from Latin primus for first, the grape is among the earliest-ripening of all varieties. The wines are typically dense and dark in colour with plenty of alcohol, and have an earthy, spicy style. Often a real bargain.

Prosecco – White grape variety of Italy's Veneto region known entirely for the softly sparkling wine it makes. The best come from the DOC Conegliano-Valdobbiadene, made as spumante ('foaming') wines in pressurised tanks, typically to 11 per cent alcohol and ranging from softly sweet to crisply dry. Now trendy, but the cheap wines – one leading brand comes in a can – are of very variable quality.

Puglia – The region occupying the 'heel' of southern Italy, lately making many good, inexpensive wines from indigenous grape varieties.

Q

QbA – German, standing for Qualitätswein bestimmter Anbaugebiete. It means 'quality wine from designated areas' and implies that the wine is made from grapes with a minimum level of ripeness, but it's by no means a guarantee of exciting quality. Only wines labelled QmP (see next entry) can be depended upon to be special.

QmP – Stands for Qualitätswein mit Prädikat. These are the serious wines of Germany, made without the addition of sugar to 'improve' them. To qualify for QmP status, the grapes must reach a level of ripeness as measured on a sweetness scale – all according to Germany's fiendishly complicated wine-quality regulations. Wines from grapes that reach the stated minimum level of sweetness qualify for the description of Kabinett. The next level up earns the rank of Spätlese, meaning 'late-picked'. Kabinett wines can be expected to be dry and brisk in style, and Spätlese wines a little bit riper and fuller. The next grade up, Auslese, meaning 'selected harvest', indicates a wine made from super-ripe grapes; it will be golden in colour and honeyed in flavour. A generation ago, these wines were as valued, and as expensive, as any of the world's grandest appellations, but the collapse in demand for German wines in the UK – brought about by the disrepute rightly earned for floods of filthy Liebfraumilch – means they are now seriously undervalued.

Quincy – AC of Loire Valley, France, known for pebbly-dry white wines from Sauvignon grapes. The wines are forever compared to those of nearby and much better-known Sancerre – and Quincy often represents better value for money. Pronounced 'KAN-see'.

Quinta – Portuguese for farm or estate. It precedes the names of many of Portugal's best-known wines. It is pronounced 'KEEN-ta'.

R

racy – Evocative wine-tasting description for wine that thrills the tastebuds with a rush of exciting sensations. Good Rieslings often qualify.

raisiny – Wines from grapes that have been very ripe or overripe at harvest can take on a smell and flavour akin to the concentrated, heat-dried sweetness of raisins. As a minor element in the character of a wine, this can add to the appeal but as a dominant characteristic it is a fault.

rancio – Spanish term harking back to Roman times when wines were commonly stored in jars outside, exposed to the sun, so they oxidised and took on a burnt sort of flavour. Today, rancio describes a baked – and by no means unpleasant – flavour in fortified wines, particularly sherry and Madeira.

Reserva – In Portugal and Spain, this has genuine significance. The Portuguese use it for special wines with a higher alcohol level and longer ageing, although the precise periods vary between regions. In Spain, especially in the Navarra and Rioja regions, it means the wine must have had at least a year in oak and two in bottle before release.

reserve – On French (as réserve) or other wines, this implies special-quality, longer-aged wines, but has no official significance.

Retsina – The universal white wine of Greece. It has been traditionally made in Attica, the region of Athens, for a very long time, and is said to owe its origins and name to the ancient custom of sealing amphorae (terracotta jars) of the wine with a gum made from pine resin. Some of the flavour of the resin inevitably transmitted itself into the wine, and ancient Greeks acquired a lasting taste for it.

Reuilly – AC of Loire Valley, France, for crisp dry whites from Sauvignon grapes. Pronounced 'RER-yee'.

Ribatejo – Emerging wine region of Portugal. Worth seeking out on labels of red wines in particular, because new winemakers are producing lively stuff from distinctive indigenous grapes such as Castelao and Trincadeira.

Ribera del Duero – Classic wine region of north-west Spain lying along the River Duero (which crosses the border to become Portugal's Douro, forming the valley where port comes from). It is home to an estate rather oddly named Vega Sicilia, where red wines of epic quality are made and sold at equally epic prices. Further down the scale, some very good reds are made, too.

Riesling – The noble grape variety of Germany. It is correctly pronounced 'REEZ-ling', not 'RICE-ling'. Once notorious as the grape behind all those boring 'medium' Liebfraumilches and Niersteiners, this grape has had a bad press. In fact, there has never been much, if any, Riesling in Germany's cheap-and-nasty plonks. But the country's best wines, the so-called Qualitätswein mit Prädikat grades, are made almost exclusively with Riesling. These wines range from crisply fresh and appley styles to extravagantly fruity, honeyed wines from late-harvested grapes. Excellent Riesling wines are also made in Alsace and now in Australia.

Rioja – The principal fine-wine region of Spain, in the country's north east. The pricier wines are noted for their vanilla-pod richness from long ageing in oak casks. Tempranillo and Garnacha grapes make the reds, Viura the whites.

Ripasso – A particular style of Valpolicella wine. New wine is partially refermented in vats that have been used to make the recioto reds (wines made from semi-dried grapes), thus creating a bigger, smoother version of usually light and pale Valpolicella.

Riserva – In Italy, a wine made only in the best vintages, and allowed longer ageing in cask and bottle.

Rivaner – Alternative name for Germany's Müller-Thurgau grape, the life-blood of Liebfraumilch.

Riverland – Vineyard region to the immediate north of the Barossa Valley of South Australia, extending east into New South Wales.

Roditis – White grape variety of Greece, known for fresh dry whites with decent acidity, often included in retsina.

rosso – Red wine, Italy.

Rosso Conero – DOC red wine made in the environs of Ancona in the Marches, Italy. Made from the Montepulciano grape, the wine can provide excellent value for money.

Ruby Cabernet – Black grape variety of California, created by crossing Cabernet Sauvignon and Carignan. Makes soft and squelchy red wine at home and in South Africa.

Rueda – DO of north-west Spain making first-class refreshing dry whites from the indigenous Verdejo grape, imported Sauvignon, and others. Exciting quality, and prices are keen.

Rully – AC of Chalonnais region of southern Burgundy, France. White wines from Chardonnay and red wines from Pinot Noir grapes. Both can be very good and are substantially cheaper than their more northerly Burgundian neighbours. Pronounced 'ROO-yee'.

S

Saint Emilion – AC of Bordeaux, France. Centred on the romantic hill town of St Emilion, this famous sub-region makes some of the grandest red wines of France, but also some of the best-value ones. Less fashionable than the Médoc region on the opposite (west) bank of the River Gironde that bisects Bordeaux, St Emilion wines are made largely with the Merlot grape, and are relatively quick to mature. The grandest wines are classified *1er grand cru classé* and are madly expensive, but many more are classified respectively *grand cru classé* and *grand cru*, and these designations can be seen as a fairly trustworthy indicator of quality. There are several 'satellite' St Emilion ACs named after the villages at their centres, notably Lussac St Emilion, Montagne St Emilion and Puisseguin St Emilion. Some excellent wines are made by estates within these ACs, and at relatively affordable prices thanks to the comparatively humble status of their satellite designations.

Salento – Up-and-coming wine region of southern Italy. Many good bargain reds from local grapes including Nero d'Avola and Primitivo.

Sancerre – AC of the Loire Valley, France, renowned for flinty-fresh Sauvignon whites and rarer Pinot Noir reds. These wines are never cheap, and recent tastings make it plain that only the best-made, individual-producer wines are worth the money. Budget brands seem mostly dull.

Sangiovese – The local black grape of Tuscany, Italy. It is the principal variety used for Chianti and is now widely planted in Latin America – often making delicious, Chianti-like wines with characteristic cherryish-but-deeply-ripe fruit and a dry, clean finish. Chianti wines have become (unjustifiably) expensive in recent years and cheaper Italian wines such as those called Sangiovese di Toscana make a consoling substitute.

Saumur – Town and appellation of Loire Valley, France. Characterful minerally red wines from Cabernet Franc grapes, and some whites. The once-popular sparkling wines from Chenin Blanc grapes are now little seen in Britain.

Saumur-Champigny – Separate appellation for red wines from Cabernet Franc grapes of Saumur in the Loire, sometimes very good and lively.

Sauvignon Blanc – French white grape variety now grown worldwide. New Zealand is successfully challenging the long supremacy of French ACs such as Sancerre. The wines are characterised by aromas of gooseberry, fresh-cut grass, even asparagus. Flavours are often described as 'grassy' or 'nettly'.

sec – Dry wine style. French.

secco – Dry wine style. Italian.

Semillon – White grape variety originally of Bordeaux, where it is blended with Sauvignon Blanc to make fresh dry whites and, when harvested very late in the season, the ambrosial sweet whites of Barsac, Sauternes and other appellations. Even in the driest wines, the grape can be recognised from its honeyed, sweet-pineapple, even banana-like aromas. Now widely planted in Australia and Latin America, and frequently blended with Chardonnay to make dry whites, some of them interesting.

sherry – The great aperitif wine of Spain, centred on the Andalusian city of Jerez (from which the name 'sherry' is an English mispronunciation). There is a lot of sherry-style wine in the world, but only the authentic wine from Jerez and the neighbouring producing towns of Puerta de Santa Maria and Sanlucar de Barrameda may label their wines as such. The Spanish drink real sherry – very dry and fresh, pale in colour and served well-chilled – called fino and manzanilla, and darker but naturally dry variations called amontillado, palo cortado and oloroso.

Shiraz – Australian name for the Syrah grape. The variety is the most widely planted of any in Australia, and makes red wines of wildly varying quality, characterised by dense colour, high alcohol, spicy fruit and generous, cushiony texture.

Somontano – Wine region of north-east Spain. Name means 'under the mountains' – in this case the Pyrenees – and the region has had DO status since 1984. Much innovative winemaking here, with New World styles emerging. Some very good buys. A region to watch.

souple – French wine-tasting term that translates into English as 'supple' or even 'docile' as in 'pliable', but I understand it in the vinous context to mean muscular but soft – a wine with tannin as well as soft fruit.

Spätlese – *See* QmP.

spirity – Some wines, mostly from the New World, are made from grapes so ripe at harvest that their high alcohol content can be detected through a mildly burning sensation on the tongue, similar to the effect of sipping a spirit.

spritzy – Describes a wine with a barely detectable sparkle. Some young wines are intended to have this elusive fizziness; in others it is a fault.

spumante – Sparkling wine of Italy. Asti Spumante is the best known, from the town of Asti in the north-west Italian province of Piemonte. The term describes wines that are fully sparkling. Frizzante wines have a less vigorous mousse.

stalky – A useful tasting term to describe red wines with flavours that make you think the stalks from the grape bunches must have been fermented along with the must (juice). Young Bordeaux reds very often have this mild astringency. In moderation it's fine, but if it dominates it probably signifies the wine is at best immature and at worst badly made.

Stellenbosch – Town and region at the heart of South Africa's burgeoning wine industry. It's an hour's drive from Cape Town and the source of much of the country's cheaper wine. Quality is variable, and the name Stellenbosch on a label can't (yet, anyway) be taken as a guarantee of quality.

stony – Wine-tasting term for keenly dry white wines. It's meant to indicate a wine of purity and real quality, with just the right match of fruit and acidity.

structured – Good wines are not one-dimensional, they have layers of flavour and texture. A structured wine has phases of enjoyment: the 'attack', or first impression in the mouth; the middle palate as the wine is held in the mouth; and the lingering aftertaste.

summer fruit – Wine-tasting term intended to convey a smell or taste of soft fruits such as strawberries and raspberries – without having to commit too specifically to which.

Superiore – On labels of Italian wines, this is more than an idle boast. Under DOC rules, wines must qualify for the Superiore designation by reaching one or more specified quality levels, usually a higher alcohol content or an additional period of maturation. Frascati, for example, qualifies for DOC status at 11.5 per cent alcohol, but to be classified Superiore must have 12 per cent alcohol.

sur lie – Literally, 'on the lees'. It's a term now widely used on the labels of Muscadet wines, signifying that after fermentation has died down, the new wine has been left in the tank over the winter on the lees – the detritus of yeasts and other interesting compounds left over from the turbid fermentation process. The idea is that additional interest is imparted into the flavour of the wine.

Syrah – The noble grape of the Rhône Valley, France. Makes very dark, dense wine characterised by peppery, tarry aromas. Now planted all over southern France and farther afield. In Australia, where it makes wines ranging from disagreeably jam-like plonks to wonderfully rich and silky keeping wines, it is known as Shiraz.

T

table wine – Wine that is unfortified and of an alcoholic strength, for UK tax purposes anyway, of no more than 15 per cent. I use the term to distinguish, for example, between the red table wines of the Douro Valley in Portugal and the region's better-known fortified wine, port.

Tafelwein – Table wine, German. The humblest quality designation, which doesn't usually bode very well.

tank method – Bulk-production process for sparkling wines. Base wine undergoes secondary fermentation in a large, sealed vat rather than in individual closed bottles. Also known as the Charmat method after the name of the inventor of the process.

Tannat – Black grape of south-west France, notably for wines of Madiran, and lately named as the variety most beneficial to health thanks to its outstanding antioxidant content.

tannin – Well known as the film-forming, teeth-coating component in tea, tannin is a natural compound that occurs in black grape skins and acts as a natural preservative in wine. Its noticeable presence in wine is regarded as a good thing. It gives young everyday reds their dryness, firmness of flavour and backbone. And it helps high-quality reds to retain their lively fruitiness for many years. A grand Bordeaux red when first made, for example, will have purply-sweet, rich fruit and mouth-puckering tannin, but after ten years or so this will have evolved into a delectably fruity, mature wine in which the formerly parching effects of the tannin have receded almost completely, leaving the shade of 'residual tannin' that marks out a great wine approaching maturity.

Tarrango – Black grape variety of Australia.

tarry – On the whole, winemakers don't like critics to say their wines evoke the redolence of road repairs, but I can't help using this term to describe the agreeable, sweet, 'burnt' flavour that is often found at the centre of the fruit in wines from Argentina, Italy and Portugal in particular.

TCA – Dreaded ailment in wine, usually blamed on faulty corks. It stands for 246 *trichloroanisol* and is characterised by a horrible musty smell and flavour in the affected wine. It is largely because of the current plague of TCA that so many wine producers worldwide are now going over to polymer 'corks' and screwcaps.

tears – The colourless alcohol in the wine left clinging to the inside of the glass after the contents have been swirled. Persistent tears (also known as 'legs') indicate a wine of good concentration.

Tempranillo – The great black grape of Spain. Along with Garnacha (Grenache in France) it makes all red Rioja and Navarra wines and, under many pseudonyms, is an important or exclusive contributor to the wines of many other regions of Spain. It is also widely cultivated in South America.

tinto – On Spanish labels indicates a deeply coloured red wine. Clarete denotes a paler colour. Also Portuguese.

Toro – Quality wine region east of Zamora, Spain.

Torrontes – White grape variety of Argentina. Makes soft, dry wines often with delicious grapey-spicy aroma, similar in style to the classic dry Muscat wines of Alsace, but at more accessible prices.

Touraine – Region encompassing a swathe of the Loire Valley, France. Non-AC wines may be labelled 'Sauvignon de Touraine' etc.

Touriga Nacional – The most valued black grape variety of the Douro Valley in Portugal, where port is made. The name Touriga now appears on an increasing number of table wines made as sidelines by the port producers. They can be very good, with the same spirity aroma and sleek flavours of port itself, minus the fortification.

Traminer – Grape variety, the same as Gewürztraminer.

Trebbiano – The workhorse white grape of Italy. A productive variety that is easy to cultivate, it seems to be included in just about every ordinary white wine of the entire nation – including Frascati, Orvieto and Soave. It is the same grape as France's Ugni Blanc. There are, however, distinct regional variations of the grape. Trebbiano di Lugana makes a distinctive white in the DOC of the name, sometimes very good, while Trebbiano di Toscana makes a major contribution to the distinctly less interesting dry whites of Chianti country.

Trincadeira Preta – Portuguese black grape variety native to the port-producing vineyards of the Douro Valley (where it goes under the name Tinta Amarella). In southern Portugal, it produces dark and sturdy table wines.

trocken – 'Dry' German wine. It's a recent trend among commercial-scale producers in the Rhine and Mosel to label their wines with this description in the hope of reassuring consumers that the contents do not resemble the dreaded sugar-water Liebfraumilch-type plonks of the bad old days. But the description does have a particular meaning under German wine law, namely that there is only a low level of unfermented sugar lingering in the wine (9 grams per litre, if you need to know), and this can leave the wine tasting rather austere.

U

Ugni Blanc – The most widely cultivated white grape variety of France and the mainstay of many a cheap dry white wine. To date it has been better known as the provider of base wine for distilling into armagnac and cognac, but lately the name has been appearing on wine labels. Technology seems to be improving the performance of the grape. The curious name is pronounced 'OON-yee', and is the same variety as Italy's ubiquitous Trebbiano.

V

Vacqueyras – Village of the southern Rhône Valley of France in the region better known for its generic appellation, the Côtes du Rhône. Vacqueyras can date its winemaking history all the way back to 1414, but has only been producing under its own village AC since 1991. The wines, from Grenache and Syrah grapes, can be wonderfully silky and intense, spicy and long-lived.

Valdepeñas – An island of quality production amidst the ocean of mediocrity that is Spain's La Mancha region – where most of the grapes are grown for distilling into the head-banging brandies of Jerez. Valdepeñas reds are made from a grape they call the Cencibel – which turns out to be a very close relation of the Tempranillo grape that is the mainstay of the fine but expensive red wines of Rioja. Again, like Rioja, Valdepeñas wines are matured in oak casks to give them a vanilla-rich smoothness. Among bargain reds, Valdepeñas is a name to look out for.

Valpolicella – Red wine of Verona, Italy. Good examples have ripe, cherry fruit and a pleasingly dry finish. Unfortunately, there are many bad examples of Valpolicella. Shop with circumspection. Valpolicella Classico wines, from the best vineyards clustered around the town, are more reliable. Those additionally labelled Superiore have higher alcohol and some bottle age.

vanilla – Ageing wines in oak barrels (or, less picturesquely, adding oak chips to wine in huge concrete vats) imparts a range of characteristics including a smell of vanilla from the ethyl vanilline naturally given off by oak.

varietal – A varietal wine is one named after the grape variety (one or more) from which it is made. Nearly all everyday wines worldwide are now labelled in this way. It is salutary to contemplate that just 30 years ago, wines described thus were virtually unknown outside Germany and one or two quirky regions of France and Italy.

vegan-friendly – My informal way of noting that a wine is claimed to have been made not only with animal-product-free finings (*see* Vegetarian wine) but without any animal-related products whatsoever, such as manure in the vineyards.

vegetal – A tasting note definitely open to interpretation. It suggests a smell or flavour reminiscent less of fruit (apple, pineapple, strawberry and the like) than of something leafy or even root based. Some wines are evocative (to some tastes) of beetroot, cabbage or even unlikelier vegetable flavours – and these characteristics may add materially to the attraction of the wine.

vegetarian wine – Wines labelled 'suitable for vegetarians' have been made without the assistance of animal products for 'fining' – clarifying – before bottling. Gelatine, egg whites, isinglass from fish bladders and casein from milk are among the items shunned, usually in favour of bentonite, an absorbent clay first found at Benton in the US state of Montana.

Verdejo – White grape of the Rueda region in north-west Spain. It can make superbly perfumed crisp dry whites of truly distinctive character and has helped make Rueda one of the best white-wine sources of Europe. No relation to Verdelho.

Verdelho – Portuguese grape variety once mainly used for a medium-dry style of Madeira, also called Verdelho, but now rare. The vine is now prospering in Australia, where it can make well-balanced dry whites with fleeting richness and lemon-lime acidity.

Verdicchio – White grape variety of Italy best known in the DOC zone of Castelli dei Jesi in the Adriatic wine region of the Marches. Dry white wines once known for little more than their naff amphora-style bottles but now gaining a reputation for interesting, herbaceous flavours of recognisable character.

Vermentino – White grape variety principally of Italy, especially Sardinia. Makes florally scented soft dry whites.

Vieilles vignes – Old vines. Many French producers like to claim on their labels that the wine within is from vines of notable antiquity. While it's true that vines don't produce useful grapes for the first few years after planting, it is uncertain whether vines of much greater age – say 25 years plus – than others actually make better fruit. There are no regulations governing the use of the term, so it's not a reliable indicator anyway.

Vin Délimité de Qualité Supérieure – Usually abbreviated to VDQS, a French wine-quality designation between appellation contrôlée and vin de pays. To qualify, the wine has to be from approved grape varieties grown in a defined zone. This designation is gradually disappearing.

vin de liqueur – Sweet style of white wine mostly from the Pyrenean region of south-westernmost France, made by adding a little spirit to the new wine before it has fermented out, halting the fermentation and retaining sugar.

vin de pays – 'Country wine' of France. The French map is divided up into more than 100 vin de pays regions. Wine in bottles labelled as such must be from grapes grown in the nominated zone or département. Some vin de pays areas are huge: the Vin de Pays d'Oc (named after the Languedoc region) covers much of the Midi and Provence. Plenty of wines bearing this humble designation are of astoundingly high quality and certainly compete with New World counterparts for interest and value. *See* Indication Géographique Protégée.

vin de table – The humblest official classification of French wine. Neither the region, grape varieties nor vintage need be stated on the label. The wine might not even be French. Don't expect too much from this kind of 'table wine'.

vin doux naturel – Sweet, mildly fortified wine of southern France. A little spirit is added during the winemaking process, halting the fermentation by killing the yeast before it has consumed all the sugars – hence the pronounced sweetness of the wine.

vin gris – Rosé wine from Provence.

Vinho de mesa – 'Table wine' of Portugal.

Vino da tavola – The humblest official classification of Italian wine. Much ordinary plonk bears this designation, but the bizarre quirks of Italy's wine laws dictate that some of that country's finest wines are also classed as mere vino da tavola (table wine). If an expensive Italian wine is labelled as such, it doesn't mean it will be a disappointment.

Vino de mesa – 'Table wine' of Spain. Usually very ordinary.

vintage – The grape harvest. The year displayed on bottle labels is the year of the harvest. Wines bearing no date have been blended from the harvests of two or more years.

Viognier – A grape variety once exclusive to the northern Rhône Valley in France where it makes a very chi-chi wine, Condrieu, usually costing £20 plus. Now, the Viognier is grown more widely, in North and South America as well as elsewhere in France, and occasionally produces soft, marrowy whites that echo the grand style of Condrieu itself. The Viognier is now commonly blended with Shiraz in red winemaking in Australia and South Africa. It does not dilute the colour and is confidently believed by highly experienced winemakers to enhance the quality. Steve Webber, in charge of winemaking at the revered De Bortoli estates in the Yarra Valley region of Victoria, Australia, puts between two and five per cent Viognier in with some of his Shiraz wines. 'I think it's the perfume,' he told me. 'It gives some femininity to the wine.'

Viura – White grape variety of Rioja, Spain. Also widely grown elsewhere in Spain under the name Macabeo. Wines have a blossomy aroma and are dry, but sometimes soft at the expense of acidity.

Vouvray – AC of the Loire Valley, France, known for still and sparkling dry white wines and sweet, still whites from late-harvested grapes. The wines, all from Chenin Blanc grapes, have a unique capacity for unctuous softness combined with lively freshness – an effect best portrayed in the demi-sec (slightly sweet) wines, which can be delicious and keenly priced. Unfashionable, but worth looking out for.

Vranac – Black grape variety of the Balkans known for dense colour and tangy-bitter edge to the flavour. Best enjoyed in situ.

W

weight – In an ideal world the weight of a wine is determined by the ripeness of the grapes from which it has been made. In some cases the weight is determined merely by the quantity of sugar added during the production process. A good, genuine wine described as having weight is one in which there is plenty of alcohol and 'extract' – colour and flavour from the grapes. Wine enthusiasts judge weight by swirling the wine in the glass and then examining the 'legs' or 'tears' left clinging to the inside of the glass after the contents have subsided. Alcohol gives these runlets a dense, glycerine-like condition, and if they cling for a long time, the wine is deemed to have weight – a very good thing in all honestly made wines.

Winzergenossenschaft – One of the many very lengthy and peculiar words regularly found on labels of German wines. This means a winemaking co-operative. Many excellent German wines are made by these associations of growers.

woodsap – A subjective tasting note. Some wines have a fleeting bitterness, which is not a fault, but an interesting balancing factor amidst very ripe flavours. The effect somehow evokes woodsap.

X

Xarel-lo – One of the main grape varieties for cava, the sparkling wine of Spain.

Xinomavro – Black grape variety of Greece. It retains its acidity even in the very hot conditions that prevail in many Greek vineyards, where harvests tend to over-ripen and make cooked-tasting wines. Modern winemaking techniques are capable of making well-balanced wines from Xinomavro.

Y

Yecla – Town and DO wine region of eastern Spain, close to Alicante, making lots of interesting, strong-flavoured red and white wines, often at bargain prices.

yellow – White wines are not white at all, but various shades of yellow – or, more poetically, gold. Some white wines with opulent richness even have a flavour I cannot resist calling yellow – reminiscent of butter.

Z

Zinfandel – Black grape variety of California. Makes brambly reds, some of which can age very gracefully, and 'blush' whites – actually pink, because a little of the skin colour is allowed to leach into the must. The vine is also planted in Australia and South America. The Primitivo of southern Italy is said to be a related variety, but makes a very different kind of wine.

—*Making the most of it*—

There has always been a lot of nonsense talked about the correct ways to serve wine. Red wine, we are told, should be opened and allowed to 'breathe' before pouring. White wine should be chilled. Wine doesn't go with soup, tomatoes or chocolate. You know the sort of thing.

It would all be simply laughable except that these daft conventions do make so many potential wine lovers nervous about the simple ritual of opening a bottle and sharing it around. Here is a short and opinionated guide to the received wisdom.

Breathing

Simply uncorking a wine for an hour or two before you serve it will make absolutely no difference to the way it tastes. However, if you wish to warm up an icy bottle of red by placing it near (never on) a radiator or fire, do remove the cork first. As the wine warms, even very slightly, it gives off gas, which will spoil the flavour if it cannot escape.

Chambré-ing

One of the more florid terms in the wine vocabulary. The idea is that red wine should be at the same temperature as the room (chambre) you're going to drink it in. In fairness, it makes sense – although the term harks back to the days when the only people who drank wine were those who could afford to keep it in the freezing cold vaulted cellars beneath their houses. The ridiculously high temperatures to which some homes are raised by central heating systems today are really far too warm for wine. But presumably those who live in such circumstances do so out of choice, and will prefer their wine to be similarly overheated.

Chilling

Drink your white wine as cold as you like. It's certainly true that good whites are at their best at a cool rather than at an icy temperature, but cheap and characterless wines can be improved immeasurably if they are cold enough – the anaesthetising effect of the temperature removes all sense of taste. Pay no attention to notions that red wine should not be served cool. There are plenty of lightweight reds that will respond very well to an hour in the fridge.

Corked wine

Wine trade surveys reveal that far too many bottles are in no fit state to be sold. The villain is very often cited as the cork. Cut from the bark of cork-oak trees cultivated for the purpose in Portugal and Spain, these natural stoppers have done sterling service for 200 years, but now face a crisis of confidence among wine producers. A diseased or damaged cork can make the wine taste stale because air has penetrated, or musty-mushroomy due to TCA, an infection of the raw material. These faults in wine, known as 'corked' or 'corky', should be immediately obvious, even in the humblest bottle, so you should return the bottle to the supplier and demand a refund.

Today, more and more wine producers are opting to close their bottles with polymer bungs. Some are designed to resemble the 'real thing' while others come in a rather disorienting range of colours – including black. While these things can be a pain to extract, there seems to be no evidence they do any harm to the wine. Don't 'lay down' bottles closed with polymer. The potential effects of years of contact with the plastic are yet to be scientifically established.

The same goes for screwcaps. These do have the merit of obviating the struggle with the corkscrew, but prolonged contact of the plastic liner with the wine might not be a good idea.

Corkscrews

The best kind of corkscrew is the 'waiter's friend' type. It looks like a pen-knife, unfolding a 'worm' (the helix or screw) and a lever device which, after the worm has been driven into the cork (try to centre it) rests on the lip of the bottle and enables you to withdraw the cork with minimal effort. Some have two-stage lips to facilitate the task. These devices are cheaper and longer-lasting than any of the more elaborate types, and are equally effective at withdrawing polymer bungs – which can be hellishly difficult to unwind from Teflon-coated 'continuous' corkscrews like the Screwpull.

Decanting

There are two views on the merits of decanting wines. The prevailing one seems to be that it is pointless and even pretentious. The other is that it can make real improvements in the way a wine tastes and is definitely worth the trouble.

Scientists, not usually much exercised by the finer nuances of wine, will tell you that exposure to the air causes wine to 'oxidise' – take in oxygen molecules that will quite quickly initiate the process of turning wine into vinegar – and anyone who has tasted a 'morning-after' glass of wine will no doubt vouch for this.

But the fact that wine does oxidise is a genuine clue to the reality of the effects of exposure to air. Shut inside its bottle, a young wine is very much a live substance, jumping with natural, but mysterious, compounds that can cause all sorts of strange taste sensations. But by exposing the wine to air these effects are markedly reduced.

In wines that spend longer in the bottle, the influence of these factors diminishes, in a process called 'reduction'. In red wines, the hardness of tannin – the natural preservative imparted into wine from the grape skins – gradually reduces, just as the raw purple colour darkens to ruby and later to orangey-brown.

I believe there is less reason for decanting old wines than new, unless the old wine has thrown a deposit and needs carefully to be poured off it. And in some light-bodied wines, such as older Rioja, decanting is probably a bad idea because it can accelerate oxidation all too quickly.

As to actual experiments, I have carried out several of my own, with wines opened in advance or wines decanted compared to the same wines just opened and poured, and my own unscientific judgement is that big, young, alcoholic reds can certainly be improved by aeration.

Washing glasses

If your wine glasses are of any value to you, don't put them in the dishwasher. Over time, they'll craze from the heat of the water. And they will not emerge in the glitteringly pristine condition suggested by the pictures on some detergent packets. For genuinely perfect glasses that will stay that way, wash them in hot soapy water, rinse with clean, hot water and dry immediately with a glass cloth kept exclusively for this purpose. Sounds like fanaticism, but if you take your wine seriously, you'll see there is sense in it.

Keeping wine

How long can you keep an opened bottle of wine before it goes downhill? Not long. A re-corked bottle with just a glassful out of it should stay fresh until the day after, but if there is a lot of air inside the bottle, the wine will oxidise, turning progressively stale and sour. Wine 'saving' devices that allow you to withdraw the air from the bottle via a punctured, self-sealing rubber stopper are variably effective, but don't expect these to keep a wine fresh for more than a couple of re-openings. A crafty method of keeping a half-finished bottle is to decant it, via a funnel, into a clean half bottle and recork.

Storing wine

Supermarket labels always seem to advise that 'this wine should be consumed within one year of purchase'. I think this is a wheeze to persuade customers to drink it up quickly and come back for more. Many of the more robust red wines are likely to stay in good condition for much more than one year, and plenty will actually improve with age. On the other hand, it is a sensible axiom that inexpensive dry white wines are better the younger they are. If you do intend to store wines for longer than a few weeks, do pay heed to the conventional wisdom that bottles are best stored in low, stable temperatures, preferably in the dark. Bottles closed with conventional corks should be laid on their side lest the corks dry out for lack of contact with the wine. But one of the notable advantages of the new closures now proliferating is that if your wine comes with a polymer 'cork' or a screwcap, you can safely store it upright.

Wine and food

Wine is made to be drunk with food, but some wines go better with particular dishes than others. It is no coincidence that Italian wines, characterised by soft, cherry fruit and a clean, mouth-drying finish, go so well with the sticky delights of pasta.

But it's personal taste rather than national associations that should determine the choice of wine with food. And if you prefer a black-hearted Argentinian Malbec to a brambly Italian Barbera with your Bolognese, that's fine.

The conventions that have grown up around wine and food pairings do make some sense, just the same. I was thrilled to learn in the early days of my drinking career that sweet, dessert wines can go well with strong blue cheese. As I don't much like puddings, but love sweet wines, I was eager to test this match – and I'm here to tell you that it works very well indeed as the end-piece to a grand meal in which there is cheese as well as pud on offer.

Red wine and cheese are supposed to be a natural match, but I'm not so sure. Reds can taste awfully tinny with soft cheeses such as Brie and Camembert, and even worse with goat's cheese. A really extravagant, yellow Australian Chardonnay will make a better match. Hard cheeses such as Cheddar and the wonderful Old Amsterdam (top-of-the-market Gouda) are better with reds.

And then there's the delicate issue of fish. Red wine is supposed to be a no-no. This might well be true of grilled and wholly unadorned white fish, such as sole or a delicate dish of prawns, scallops or crab. But what about oven-roasted monkfish or a substantial winter-season fish pie? An edgy red will do very well indeed, and provide much comfort for those many among us who simply prefer to drink red wine with food, and white wine on its own.

It is very often the method by which dishes are prepared, rather than their core ingredients, that determines which wine will work best. To be didactic, I would always choose Beaujolais or summer-fruit-style reds such as those from Pinot Noir grapes to go with a simple roast chicken. But if the bird is cooked as coq au vin with a hefty wine sauce, I would plump for a much more assertive red.

Some sauces, it is alleged, will overwhelm all wines. Salsa and curry come to mind. I have carried out a number of experiments into this great issue of our time, in my capacity as consultant to a company that specialises in supplying wines to Asian restaurants. One discovery I have made is that forcefully fruity dry white wines with keen acidity can go very well indeed even with fairly incendiary dishes. Sauvignon Blanc with Madras? Give it a try!

I'm also convinced, however, that some red wines will stand up very well to a bit of heat. The marvellously robust reds of Argentina made from Malbec grapes are good partners to Mexican chilli-hot recipes and salsa dishes. The dry, tannic edge to these wines provides a good counterpoint to the inflammatory spices in the food.

Some foods are supposedly impossible to match with wine. Eggs and chocolate are among the prime offenders. And yet, legendary cook Elizabeth David's best-selling autobiography was entitled *An Omelette and a Glass of Wine*, and the affiliation between chocolates and champagne is an unbreakable one. Taste is, after all, that most personally governed of all senses. If your choice is a boiled egg washed down with a glass of claret, who is to dictate otherwise?

Index